SHORTCUT YO

Courtney and Carter Reum are en
Goldman Sachs investment bankers.
successfully selling VEEV Spirits, Co
investing platform that specialises in scaling consumer
Together they have invested in companies ranging from Lyft to Pinterest
to SpaceX. They currently live in Los Angeles, where they run day-to-day
operations at M13.

Praise for *Shortcut Your Startup*

'The Internet's Third Wave is upon us. *Shortcut Your Startup* is a helpful guide for entrepreneurs who want to lead the way.' Steve Case, co-founder and CEO of AOL

'Cultivating relationships is one of the keys to business success. In *Shortcut Your Startup*, Courtney and Carter share the best insights from their own ventures as well as what they've learned through their vast network.' Keith Ferrazzi, author of *Never Eat Alone*

'*Shortcut Your Startup* is the handbook for the future founders of the world's culturally relevant brands. It is hands down a must-read for consumer products entrepreneurs and anyone thinking of starting a business in today's media and technology-driven landscape.' Troy Carter, former Global Head of Creator Services at Spotify

'Want to be an entrepreneur? You sure? Here is a great test/checklist/guide from two great startup gurus who have been there and done that . . .' Professor Juan Enríquez, Harvard Business School

Shortcut Your Startup

Ten Ways to Speed Up
Entrepreneurial Success

Courtney and Carter Reum

BUSINESS
BOOKS

1 3 5 7 9 10 8 6 4 2

Random House Business Books
20 Vauxhall Bridge Road
London SW1V 2SA

Random House Business Books is part of the Penguin Random House group of
companies whose addresses can be found at global.penguinrandomhouse.com.

Penguin
Random House
UK

First published in the United Kingdom by Random House Business Books in 2018
First published in the United States by Gallery in 2018
This edition first published by Random House Business Books in 2019

www.penguin.co.uk

A CIP catalogue record for this book is available from the British Library.

ISBN 9781847942319

Printed and bound in Great Britain by Clays Ltd, Elcograf S.p.A.

Penguin Random House is committed to a sustainable future
for our business, our readers and our planet. This book is made
from Forest Stewardship Council® certified paper.

MIX
Paper from
responsible sources
FSC® C018179

Dedication

This book was always going to be very personal for us. We've never put anything out into the world quite like this, and we may never do so again.

However, shortly after we started writing this book, everything in our lives changed. Our father, W. Robert Reum, passed away very suddenly and unexpectedly. More than anything, he was the patriarch of our family, our oldest friend as well as an incredibly loving father and husband. He was an exemplary human being.

As devastated as we've been, we know that he would want us still to "pull it together" (as he used to say) and make this book that much better. So that's what we've attempted to do.

Beyond that, the book has given us a chance to reflect on our father's influence on us as businessmen and entrepreneurs. Over the last decade, we started to share some business ventures with Dad. It was truly special to be able to learn from such a strong and humble leader and, occasionally, to be able to teach him something, too.

Our dad was all about the fundamentals and the universal truths of both business and life. We know what he would say if he read our book: "Of course I'm proud of you and this new world. Information 2.0 is great, but it's irrelevant if you don't get the basics right: strategy, execution, and people."

He was absolutely right. He pretty much always was, and we wish we'd told him that more often. If you do everything in our book but get the foundation wrong, everything we've tried to espouse will be for naught. We hear you, Dad—and we agree.

This book is dedicated to our dad. We are so grateful and love you so much.

Contents

It's a Whole New Startup World Out There, and Time Is Your Scarcest Resource

You've picked up this book because you're an entrepreneur—or are thinking about becoming one. Welcome to the faster, more complicated, and ever more competitive startup landscape.

Through the Internet, new distribution models, and abundant access to information and capital, the barriers to entry for entrepreneurs have dropped and the floodgates have opened. It's easier and less expensive to start a business in today's market than it has ever been, and entrepreneurs are taking full advantage of this opportunity. Over the last twenty years, the cost of launching a new business has come down by a factor of nearly 100, due largely to the proliferation of open source tools and the Internet's many applications to allow entrepreneurs to start some businesses today for as little as $5,000. These same forces are also creating a more crowded environment in which it is more challenging to compete and grow. The old ways of running a business are less impactful. The traditional methods of starting and scaling are too cumbersome, costly, and slow.

Today, the companies that win are those that move more quickly and flexibly than their competitors. This new environment requires new strategies, new mind-sets, and new tactics to shorten timelines, stand out, and win. That's what this book is about.

Within these pages, we share with you our approach to succeeding in today's sped-up startup world, featuring ten "Startup Switchups" that flip typical startup advice on its head. One Switchup at a time, we take you through our insights on what's new at each stage of a venture—and show you proven strategies to help you develop a crucial edge over the competition. We hope that what you learn in these pages will open your mind and fundamentally change how you think about starting and growing your company.

We're brothers who know the brave new startup world firsthand. As former Goldman Sachs investment bankers, we first watched businesses get built through the lens of corporate finance and then made our jump, building a business from inception to sale. Now, as operators and VCs at our new venture capital and brand development company, M13, we take a portfolio approach and still get our hands dirty. We've played various positions in growing great brands and have been fortunate to support notable modern brands, including Bonobos, Lyft, Warby Parker, Class-Pass, and more than a hundred others.

In our careers, we've spent the most time as entrepreneurs. Creating VEEV, a consumer spirits company, in 2007 from the ground up, we went from 0 to 60 in less than a decade: seeing the market opportunity for an all-natural, eco-friendly vodka, developing the product, selling the product out of the back of our car, building our customer base, marketing the product nationally, creating brand extensions, and successfully selling the business to a larger company. In doing so, we learned a tremendous amount about launching and growing a consumer products business as well as many of the avoidable pitfalls. In this book, we'll share with you some of the dos and don'ts we learned from our firsthand experience.

Whether you are opening an e-commerce store or a physical boutique, the tools and information that you need to get started are at your fingertips. As Steve Case, the former CEO of AOL, put it, "The exciting part about living today is that anyone can be an entrepreneur." We're living in a world where information is not just readily available but, in many cases, overwhelming. Building a business from the ground up is not easy; that's why we're here: to help you cut through some of the noise and provide some advice garnered from our experience as both operators and investors.

We want you to better understand what the forces of globalization and innovation mean for you and your business, whether your startup is just a thought in your head or a living, breathing entity. To increase your odds of success, we'll be sharing the unconventional tricks of the trade we've gained both personally and from many of the successful entrepreneurs we've been lucky to work with and learn from.

Though entrepreneurship is uniquely challenging, there may have never been a better, or more important, time to take the leap. Entrepreneurs are world evolvers whom we need to help us progress in all sectors of society. As Eric Schmidt, the executive chairman of Alphabet and someone we respect very much, says, "[Entrepreneurs] are people who somehow believe that they can make the world different and better, and they're willing to take their own lives, their own time, and so forth, and their own risk capital, and put it together to create literally millions of jobs and ultimately trillions of dollars of wealth." Entrepreneurship is by no means easy, but we hope this book will help you overcome the inevitable obstacles and become one of the game changers.

COMPETITION IS FIERCE

How competitive is it out there? According to a recent survey, an estimated 550,000 new businesses open in the United States each month. Unfortunately, the competition is too fierce for all of those businesses to survive, and many do not. The intense competition is not limited to the startup world. The S&P 500 Index showcases a dramatic fall in the average life-span of even the most well-established companies—from sixty years a few decades ago to twenty years today. In other words, competition is rampant throughout today's economy, and it is forcing companies large and small to evolve or die more quickly than ever. Let's do a deeper analysis to understand what's happening and how it impacts your business.

RAPID BRAND BUILDING

When we were at Goldman, Kevin Plank, the founder of Under Armour, who was one of our earliest inspirations, spoke to us about the minimum amount of time it takes to build a brand, which he said at the time was approximately ten years. That made sense. People needed to be exposed to a product or service multiple times and in a variety of settings in order to create strong and—hopefully—positive associations. We saw that with VEEV, and, until recently, we thought that Kevin's rule still held true. However, this is often no longer the case.

Just as startup companies are both emerging and failing at unprecedented rates, brand building is no longer a decade-plus process. The amount of time that it takes to build a recognizable brand, a "household name," has been dramatically reduced. One key indicator of this is the rate at which today's companies are scaling. (See the chart below.)

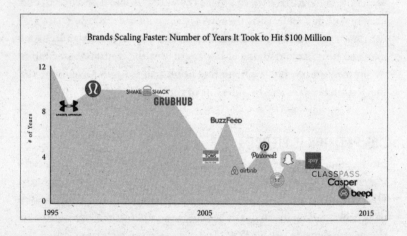

As Mary Meeker pointed out in her 2016 *Internet Trends Report*, it took Nike fourteen years to reach $100 million in sales, Lululemon nine years, and Under Armour eight. At the time, those brands were some of the fastest-growing consumer brands around. They were—and remain—massive successes. However, in the last few years, we've seen tech-enabled consumer brands such as ClassPass, Dollar Shave Club,

Casper, and the Honest Company reach the same heights in significantly less time. (And fall equally fast—Beepi, established in 2013, was out of business by 2017.)

We believe that five critical factors are fueling the rapid scaling of consumer brands in today's market. They combine to act as a flywheel, accelerating business life cycles.

1. Personal computers in our pockets are creating new behaviors.

It's easy to take for granted the extent to which these devices have worked their way into our waking and sleeping lives. What we used to call "smartphones" are now portable computers that we carry around with us and touch on average 2,600 times per day. Americans spend 71 percent of their total digital minutes on smartphones, and as the growth of desktops slowly plateaus, smartphone usage continues to rise. In fact, mobile Internet usage is growing at over 11 percent each year and recently hit a new high of 220 minutes per day. In contrast, in 2011, usage was under 50 minutes. In 2016, US smartphone users spent 90 percent of their time on mobile devices interacting with apps. More and more, people are able to do almost everything on their phones, from purchasing goods to ordering dry cleaning or massages.

The implications? First, people are more reachable than they have ever been, and they have the ability to make purchases conveniently without entering stores. Second, startups have easier and cheaper access to the market than ever before. As opposed to the past, when entrepreneurs faced expensive distribution networks, today vendors can easily get their products in front of consumers anywhere, anytime. Any vendor can sell through a platform such as Amazon, taking power away from the giant retailers that used to control the market. This dynamic shift has placed more power in the hands of technology platforms across industries such as gym membership (e.g., ClassPass) and ride-sharing services (Uber and Lyft).

2. Brands are speaking less *to* consumers and more *through* consumers.

As a result of the increased time spent on mobile platforms and social media, consumers in the United States, especially Millennials, have led the charge on a developing trend: sharing. Though "sharing economy" often refers to peer-to-peer platforms, there is no doubt that social media provide a medium for people to express their opinions on the goods and services they consume. Take entrepreneur Gary Vaynerchuk, for instance. We met him fairly early on when he was creating his Wine Library. It's not every day we meet another adult beverage alum who has transcended the category, but he's found tremendous success across various social and entertainment channels: his YouTube show, the #*AskGaryVee* show; and *The Gary Vaynerchuk Audio Experience* podcast. Across those channels, Gary has been able to interact with millions of customers and fans by responding to their Tweets and Instagram posts and covering topics ranging from gadgets, trends, and new products, to wine.

Whereas in the old days, if you tried a product and loved it, you might have recommended it to a few friends; today, if you post it to your Facebook or Instagram account, thousands of your friends and followers can see it in a matter of seconds. That is also why a product's ratings on Amazon or a restaurant's Yelp reviews are so impactful: consumers are making decisions based not only on what their friends post but on aggregated product reviews.

You've probably seen "growth hacks," where brands offer everything from discounts to cash rewards when you share a product or service with people in your network. Companies have picked up on the fact that more than 80 percent of consumers in today's market trust recommendations from individuals over brands. Consumers are looking more and more to friends and influencers on social media to learn about brands, products, and experiences. In fact, it is projected that in 2017, brands will increase their influencer marketing expenditures by more than 60 percent. Consumers are looking to share information and learn from one another, as opposed to directly from companies—and brands are beginning to react.

3. Tools are available to market in an increasingly targeted way.

In the old days, billboards, magazines, and previews dominated advertising strategies as companies took a "splatter" approach to advertising:

they found high-traffic channels and spent their marketing budgets on those channels. Today, as companies collect massive amounts of data on their consumers, brands are increasingly able to market to very specific groups of people. Platforms such as Facebook, Pinterest, and Instagram are a marketer's dream. They provide companies with access to specific types of customers and collect data on those individuals based on their activity. For example, Facebook retargeting allows an advertiser to target people who visited its website with different messages, depending on where they stopped in the buying process. Retargeting tends to have a much higher success rate than advertisements targeting customers for the first time. It's an obvious point, because retargeting is reaching a more qualified lead. These tools either didn't exist in the past or were prohibitively expensive and/or harder to track.

Similarly, look-alike targeting has proven to be very effective in our experience of scaling and growing brands at M13. Platforms such as Facebook allow digital marketers to define their target audiences based on previous user behavior and to compare existing customers to the Facebook universe in order to find similar users. Other companies are following suit, including Pinterest, which has its own act-alike audience targeting options. By using such tools to target customers strategically, you will develop increased deliverability, higher performance, and less list fatigue.

4. (Online) traffic is cheap.

What one considers to be cheap is of course relative, but the fact that mom-and-pop brands can now easily access specific customers and afford to advertise to them is a massive change in the marketing world. Whereas advertising used to be dominated by larger, well-capitalized brands, today smaller brands can afford to get their products in front of hundreds of thousands of qualified leads around the globe at a fraction of the historical cost and in much less time. The advantages in terms of capital efficiency and speed are tremendous, because getting your product or service in front of customers is no longer predicated on getting into retail or being able to afford prime advertising.

5. Abundant capital is available.

Today there's more capital available for venture growth than at any other time in history. There's actually over five times as much capital today earmarked for venture investment as there was in the late 1990s. Part of the increasing investment in venture capital is being led by "angels," corporations and individuals who, through crowdfunding and other methods, make early investments in startup companies. Since angels have joined the venture capital game, they have poured more and more money into the VC industry each year. Starting in 2009, the US angel investment market grew from $17 billion to $24 billion. This abundance of capital has made it easier for brands to expand and grow while incurring significant operating losses, with the goal of scaling faster and acquiring market share. However, the abundant capital that makes the funding environment more favorable for entrepreneurs is also making the world much more competitive. It's easier than ever to get out there but harder than ever to stick.

TIME IS YOUR SCARCEST RESOURCE

Such intense competition is the key reason why time is your scarcest resource. We can almost guarantee that if you've observed a market need, others have noticed it as well. As all entrepreneurs know, the faster and more efficiently you can get up and running and the quicker you can get your product or service to market, the more you can learn about your customers and their needs and the higher your odds of success.

We've all heard the adage that time is money, and in the startup world, that is particularly true. What entrepreneurs often fail to realize is that the cost of time is increasing. Even one month can make a big difference. Imagine that you test different messages and marketing campaigns on Facebook every day for thirty days: How much more will you learn than your competition that starts one month later?

Time is especially critical when it comes to raising capital. These days, if you don't show fast growth, you're not going to capture the attention, dollars, and imagination of investors. This is partly because investors see a lot of businesses, and they know how important fast execution is. They know that if you're moving slowly, even with the best product or service, it's much easier for others to copy you. They recognize that your time is their money—they're investing in your runway to launch and scale. *The longer you take, the more capital your business will need and the bigger your exit will need to be for anyone to make real money.*

To understand this important point about exits and valuations, let's take two companies: Company A and Company B. Both spend $100,000 per month and go on to sell for $10 million—a lot of money. Company A takes ten months to scale before being acquired, while Company B gets off to a slightly slower start, has trouble raising growth capital, but ultimately figures it out and is acquired after twenty months.

That ten-month difference makes a significant impact on the ultimate outcome. The internal rate of return, or IRR, is a key metric used by investors to measure the profitability of investments over time. With both companies burning through $100,000 per month and being acquired after ten and twenty months, respectively, for the same purchase price, what's the difference in IRR? Almost sixteen times. Company A's IRR is 5,730 percent, while company B's is only 366 percent. IRR isn't important just for investors; it's important for you.

OUR ENTREPRENEURIAL READINESS TEST

Before you start to move quickly, however, it's essential to consider whether you're the right person for the job of a founder. Although we loved starting a company and experienced it as both exhilarating and rewarding, this line of work is not for the faint of heart. We don't want to discourage you from building your dream, but we do have to warn you in advance that it is not easy.

The following are our top two reasons *not* to do it. We like to present them up front so that folks can really see what they are getting themselves into. Preparation is everything; going in with your eyes wide open will only make you better at what you do. We suggest that you pay close attention to the way these factors make you feel. Does your inner voice whisper, "Hmm, I'm not sure I want to do this," or are your competitive juices flowing?

1. Anyone *can* do it, but not everyone *should* do it.

"Can" and "should" are two different things. Entrepreneurship is not a gene that you are born with. If you are an entrepreneur, you have to want to be one, and want it really badly. Whether you're naturally personable, smart, or hardworking or none of the above, if you want to be successful in the startup world, you need to cultivate the following six factors and chase down the ones you don't innately have. If you're willing to do so, you are one of the people who "should" be an entrepreneur. You need to be:

- **Optimistic: Successful entrepreneurs believe they will succeed.**
  Despite the glamour that society builds around entrepreneurship, it's a ton of work, and the journey is a roller coaster. Though when you are a founder there are moments that make you feel on top of the world, there are twice as many moments of failure. You need to be able not only to roll with the punches but, more important, to get back up after you're knocked down. Being optimistic and maintaining a positive outlook are mission critical. When we started VEEV, we took a ton of risks in terms of both money and time, but we knew deep down that we would eventually make it work. We like to call this being "long-term greedy": you make tough decisions in the moment in order to reap larger benefits in the future.

- **Energetic: Successful entrepreneurs have both the drive to succeed and the stamina to make it happen.**
  Although much has changed in today's world, being an entrepreneur hasn't become any easier. This job has always involved resiliency and giving 110 percent. After all, the entrepreneurial mind-set is that every moment you spend not making your company or product better is a moment when competitors are catching

up. You must have high energy—and be able to channel that energy to achieve business milestones. You lead by example, and demonstrating high energy and focus will encourage your employees to strive to do the same. It's an indication of how passionate you are.

- **Risk-taking: Successful entrepreneurs have an unusually high risk tolerance.**
Any business venture, no matter the industry or stage of a company, involves risk. As a founder, not only do you have to be comfortable with taking risks, you have to constantly calculate the risk of each decision you make. Whether it's selecting a distributor or deciding whether to raise money, any decision you make has future implications. When we left Goldman Sachs to be entrepreneurs, many of our friends and colleagues questioned the decision: Why leave such an established firm and what seems like a safe path to a successful career to enter a world of unknowns? That is a reasonable question to ask. Although we often joke that "we were just young enough and just stupid enough to leave Goldman to become entrepreneurs," we were also interested in taking a risk, provided it was a thoughtful and strategic one.

- **Emotionally resilient: Successful entrepreneurs are able to bounce back quickly from the inevitable setbacks and disappointments.**
There's no "That was easy" button for entrepreneurship. We have yet to meet a successful person in our industry who's not failed before. You have to be able to recover from being wrong, from losing, from striking out, and keep on going.
  When we first produced VEEV, an açaí-infused spirit based on vodka, the product had the slightest yellow tint to it, which quite honestly surprised us. Over the subsequent weeks, as we started to sell VEEV to our first accounts, we noticed the color continuing to build, until it eventually looked more like lemonade than vodka. We debated a formal recall. But we weren't yet in millions of doors; we were still self-distributing. In order to work through what felt

like a major obstacle at the time, we took a two-pronged approach: sell the existing product that we had on hand while simultaneously tracking down the root of the problem. Both of those were significant challenges—we knew the product wasn't perfect, and finding the problem was hard—that could have ended our company's progress before it even started. But we're proud to say that we did both with enough aplomb to live to fight another day, which is actually more important than getting every decision right.

- **Visionary: Successful entrepreneurs are able to look ahead, see the big picture, and vividly paint a vision of the future.**
Find a piece of paper and a pen, or take out your phone and open up a blank note. Think about an entrepreneur role model. Write down the top five words that come to mind when you think of that person. If we were gambling men, which we are, we'd be willing to bet that the words "inspiration" and/or "visionary" are on your list.

  That's because the best founders see something that no one else sees, rally their troops around the vision, and take their teams on a journey that no one else would have imagined could or would be possible. When it comes to beverages and consumer packaged goods, from KeVita to Krave Jerky, we try to spot opportunities coming and be in a position to capitalize on them. That is how we started VEEV, by seeing an opportunity in the vodka space that no one else saw and jumping on it. The ability to recognize market trends and to vividly paint a picture of the future is what separates mediocre and/or lucky founders and investors from those who are consistently successful. We once heard Tony Robbins say something about this we liked. We don't recall the exact words, but the gist is: See the world as it is, not as worse than it is. See the world as you see it; make the world as you see it. In many ways, this sums up the job and challenge of the entrepreneur: to be visionary enough to see a better way of doing something but to ground that vision in reality enough to make it happen. Easier said than done!

- **Persuasive: Successful entrepreneurs have the ability to get others on board with their vision and to promote their ideas easily—you just want to buy whatever they're selling.**

As you have probably heard, being an entrepreneur means you have a part-time job as a salesman or saleswoman. To be honest, it's not really a part-time job—as a founder, you must constantly represent, talk about, and, most important, sell your company! This may sound like a difficult task, but at the heart of it is being persuasive.

According to one of our favorite philosophers, Aristotle, there are three pillars of persuasion: ethos, pathos, and logos. Ethos is an appeal to ethics, and it means convincing someone of your credibility. Pathos involves appealing to the listener's emotions—creating a feeling response. Logos is persuasion by reason. Whether you are speaking with investors, employees, or distributors, you should constantly try to get as many people on board as possible using these pillars.

With VEEV, we used all three. We developed relationships, earned trust, demonstrated goodwill, exuded passion and confidence, never accepted defeat, built our business with sound financials, and sold others on our vision. If you master these elements and combine them effectively, you will leverage your persuasive potential.

2. You don't have to be an entrepreneur to be an entrepreneur.

Do you work for a large company, a nonprofit, or a government organization and have an entrepreneurial mind-set? Are you able to think creatively within your current role? Though traditional advice might be to quit your job and start something, maybe staying put would be a better move. More than ever, institutions need people with an entrepreneurial mind-set to operate within the larger framework of their companies to create new products, processes, and platforms. Hence the rise of the intrapreneur. Across sectors today we are seeing this trend, where attempts to foster innovation are occurring internally. Those who succeed in this type of role will likely be rewarded. Entrepreneurial action and leadership are certainly not reserved for startup founders. Take Los Angeles mayor Eric Garcetti, a quintessential example of entrepreneurship applied in a less traditional context. Mayor Garcetti has applied many of the concepts in this book—from pivoting to find solutions that work to gaining buy-in with heart-based momentum to initiate change and attract talent—during his tenure as mayor. He epitomizes our belief that intrapreneurship can be a powerful mechanism for improving people's lives, whether they are your employees, your customers, or your constituents.

Another example of fostering intrapreneurship is Adobe's Kickbox initiative, through which any Adobe employee with a product or idea can receive a $1,000 prepaid credit card and participate in a two-day innovation workshop to develop and test out his or her concept. Adobe employees are sent a "red box," a physical box with tools and resources that encourages employees to define, refine, validate, and evolve their idea. If one executive within Adobe approves the idea, it is passed on to the next round of funding and development. Since its inception, more than a thousand ideas have been prototyped through this initiative. Obviously, not all companies make it as easy as Adobe does, but intrapreneurship may be the way to go.

STACKING THE ODDS IN YOUR FAVOR

Creating a successful company is not impossible—statistics say that 40 percent of startups receive funding. But the deck is stacked against you more than you know—only 10 percent survive the first year. And of those who succeed, most aren't billion-dollar unicorns but ventures that are still slugging it out every day to keep paying the bills.

Here's a reality check. The graph on the opposite page shows how many companies make it to each round of VC funding. As you can see, it's a very exclusive club. Fortunately, there are many successful companies that keep on chugging away without any VC money.

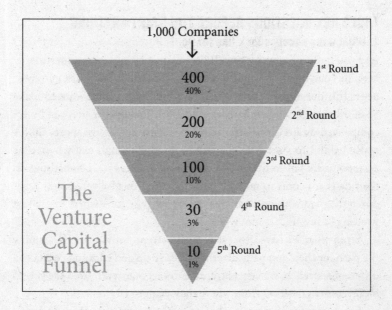

To put the odds of succeeding in the startup world into perspective, let's look at the chances of making it to the NBA. The ratio of high school basketball players who make it to the NCAA is 1 in 35, or 2.9 percent; the ratio of NCAA players who are drafted to NBA teams is 1 in 75, or 1.3 percent. Thus the odds of an NCAA basketball player making it to the NBA are higher than those of getting five rounds of funding!

If you're still reading, that's a good sign! You've passed the entrepreneurial readiness test. That probably means you're temperamentally and energetically suited for the job. That's where we come in—we can't give you the temperament, but if you have it, we can help you stack the odds so you end up in the 10 percent of folks who succeed.

Typically, success begins with a set of questions that you need to ask before you begin. If you already have a business, you should know the answers to them. If you don't, now is the time to start. Get used to them—you are likely to hear them in one form or another when you go out for funding, even at the seed stage.

THREE KEY QUESTIONS BEFORE YOU START ANYTHING
1. What does success look like for you?

Are you building a business to IPO, sell, maintain a certain lifestyle, or keep in your family for multiple generations? We always ask entrepreneurs this question because it tells us a lot. Some people want to make $2,000 a month, while others want to IPO. Though the first can be accomplished on Etsy, the latter requires a more aggressive approach. It's really helpful to start with the end in mind, although many first-time entrepreneurs fail to do so. We often see founders start something on the side that begins to take off, and they find themselves several years down the road with no clear idea of—or strategy for—where to go. Just wanting "a big IPO" is not a plan.

From what we have observed, most entrepreneurs try to determine the path for their company after it's already up and running. We take a different approach: we help entrepreneurs set out a path from the get-go by reverse engineering from where they want to land.

For instance, if your goal is to make a few thousand dollars a month, you should probably set up your business with a variable cost structure, meaning your costs are tied to your sales, versus a fixed cost structure, where your costs are an up-front investment. In a variable cost structure, you pay a bit more for everything, but you can make something on every $1 of revenue you bring in. This approach means that less up-front investment is required, since you pay expenses as you go. If, instead, you're trying to build a huge company quickly, you want a fixed cost structure, so that you will have capital reserves later when you want to expand and scale your business.

2. Why has no one else done this?

Entrepreneurs we speak with make this mistake all the time—they want to believe they're the first to have an idea. It's not that we don't see new ideas, but we've talked with many entrepreneurs who think they have a unique idea until they do some research and find that at least five other folks are already in the space. That isn't necessarily a bad thing. It's extremely rare to have a truly original idea. Remember that Uber wasn't the first ride-sharing company and Facebook wasn't the first social media platform. Being first can be a huge advantage, but being the best is more important. Being the best comes down to finding the best product/market fit—something we'll talk about throughout the book. CB Insights, an excellent source of startup research and data, reports that lack of product/market fit is one of the most cited sources of failure for startups today. If you're truly the first person on the planet with an idea, are you creating something that people actually want or need? It's possible that no one has executed the idea because there is no demand.

If you aren't creating something new, you should understand what your competitor is doing well and what the secret ingredient is that you believe they are missing. Finding this ingredient comes down to differentiation. How do you stand out from the competition and why does this make you more attractive? There are various ways to differentiate, from price point to key features and packaging. For instance, when our friend Eric Ryan, the cofounder of the pioneering eco–household products company Method Products, launched his nutrition company, Olly Nutrition, he decided to differentiate his supplements in two ways: first, by creating better packaging than existing supplements had, which was similar to what he had done with Method; second, by formulating function-driven supplements: sleep, beauty, energy, and so on.

In addition to packaging and features, you may also want to consider price points and the quality of the competitors' product and user experience. How is the competitors' product performance, and what do consumers think about it? Brand is another possible differentiator. Though your competitors may offer an amazing product and price, if the brand is weak—name, packaging, marketing, reputation—maybe you can create a highly attractive brand to dominate the space. The point is, you don't want to launch a product or service that is the same as what's already in the market!

3. Why you, and why now?
What makes you uniquely suited to doing this thing, and why is now the time to do it? Is the market ready? What are the barriers to entry?

Do you have a head start on the competition? If you are trying to go big, is the market big enough, and how will the business scale? How much runway can you get before hitting a major roadblock and serious opposition? These are important questions that you should always consider. Think about what you are best at now, and let's see how your answer evolves after reading the following chapters.

WORKING THROUGH THIS BOOK

We've organized *Shortcut Your Startup* around each stage of a venture: Part 1, "Prelaunch"; Part 2, "Running the Business"; and Part 3, "Exiting." In "Prelaunch," we begin by suggesting you get into the trenches early on to investigate the space and gain valuable insights that will help you increase your odds of success. Then we have you consider your overall business strategy and how to fund it. In Switchup 3, we help you differentiate your company to get a leg up on the competition once you're up and running. In Part 2, our Switchups focus on the day-to-day running of the business. Switchup 4 makes a case for why you should specialize through partnering and outsourcing. Switchup 5 helps you think about iteration and pivoting based on what you are learning from customers through our unique lens of a "diversified focus." Then we get more granular and tactical, teaching you our milestones approach to operational efficiency in Switchup 6; the importance of nailing your product/market fit, operating systems, and customer acquisition costs before scaling in Switchup 7; how to accelerate success through testing rigor to employ the forces of magnification in Switchup 8. We conclude this section with a deep dive into building a strong brand to win the hearts of employees and customers through a sound mission and great storytelling. Then, in Part 3, we give you our perspective on how to set yourself up to exit successfully.

We encourage you to read the whole book, no matter where you are on your startup journey. Much of what we are offering is a paradigm for thinking about startup growth and execution, and we want to make sure you have the full perspective. For instance, how you think about an exit, Switchup 10, has implications for decisions you make right from the start. And even if you've already been in business for a few years, Switchups 1 and 2 might impact your thinking about a pivot or a restructuring that could accelerate your company's growth.

Each chapter features one Switchup, organized as follows:

- The standard startup advice
- Our Switchup on that advice
- Stories of how and why our flip evolved from our personal experience, as well as from our peers in the investing and entrepreneurial world
- Concrete suggestions for how to implement the principle
- Practical tips, tricks, and techniques for greater entrepreneurial success

By the end, you will be locked and loaded with our best perspectives, advice, suggestions, and stories to take the startup world by storm. And since time is your scarcest resource, let's get started.

PART 1
PRELAUNCH

Get into the Trenches: Investigation

We learned a lot of these Switchups the hard way as entrepreneurs—and this Switchup is the perfect example. When we dived in headfirst with VEEV, trying to take our company from a startup to an established liquor brand, we had absolutely no experience in the liquor industry. We had no idea how complicated the space was.

Quickly we realized that successful entrepreneurs have a detailed idea of what they're getting into because they get out there and investigate the market, the viability of the idea, the competition, the industry dynamics, and so on, before jumping in. We call this "getting into the trenches." As soon as we figured that out, that's just what we did. We rolled up our sleeves, sold our product out of the back of our Toyota Prius, and met face-to-face with distributors, customers, and bartenders. We just wish we'd done more of that discovery work in advance. We could have avoided various mistakes, including perhaps VEEV's discoloration issue that we spoke of earlier, and been able to move faster, wasting less time (and therefore money) learning the basics. We might have even decided it wasn't the right idea for us.

Though unforeseen obstacles and hidden traps exist in any endeavor, getting into the trenches early will save a lot of headaches down the line. (As a quick aside: Cliché as it might sound, take your team to a Spartan Race or Tough Mudder. These fun and increasingly popular obstacle course races are great entrepreneurial training grounds—one obstacle after the next, each testing your mettle in a different way.) As an entrepreneur, you must minimize the number of unknowns and navigate your team around the traps to the best of your ability. Conventional wisdom says that this is done in the boardroom, setting a strategy. Our experience tells us that it is best done on the front lines, learning as much as you can before you make a big investment of time and money.

Even just a few years ago, there was less competition in the startup world, which meant that entrepreneurs had the luxury of setting strategies and slowly tinkering as they perfected them. This is no longer true. As one example, in the graph below you can see how the rate of consumer adoption is increasing every decade.

Look, for instance, at the rate of adoption for the telephone versus the cell phone. The extreme contrast is an example of how we're in a much less forgiving startup ecosystem these days. If your competitor hits it with a product, it is now able to get it in front of tens or hundreds of thousands of people in the same amount of time it would have taken in the past to get in front of thousands. The shorter rate of adoption today is what leads to a faster separation between startup winners and losers. And this is happening in an ever more crowded space. Competition is so tough that, whatever your idea, you can be sure there are a few other folks working on it, even more thinking about it, and thousands who will jump in as soon as they hear about it.

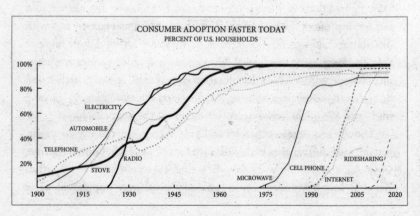

CONSUMER ADOPTION FASTER TODAY
PERCENT OF U.S. HOUSEHOLDS

The consequence? There's less time to meander. Since businesses can get their products in front of so many customers using digital tools and those customers are sharing their positive and negative experiences via social platforms, the consequences of being slow are massive. The good news is that the impact of getting it right is of an equivalent magnitude. With a solid product/market fit (PMF), you can reach more customers for less than ever before. To do so, you have to learn faster and see patterns sooner than your competition does. We believe this is best done by getting as close to the product-customer interaction in person as early as possible.

That's what this Switchup is about—focusing on the insights you can generate into product/market/timing fit when you get into the trenches early. We include timing with PMF because you can produce the right product for the right market and still fail because you land at the wrong time. If customers aren't ready for what you have to offer, you're going to spend massive amounts of money trying to acquire users in an unsustainable fashion. Though we advocate rapid execution, it's possible to be too early into the market.

The trench approach will help you save time and money, and produce the kinds of insights you need to succeed. If you've launched before doing this deep dive, you can still get out there now, armed with our ideas of what to pay attention to.

FROM THE WALL STREET TRENCHES TO THE CHIPOTLE TRENCHES

An acquaintance of ours epitomizes this Switchup. He was working at Goldman Sachs when he had an idea to do a fast casual restaurant, an Italian version of Chipotle. Traditionally, he would take one of two approaches: spend months or years researching to understand everything about the market, where to start, and what cash flows might look like; or, as a brash ex-banker, find some capital and jump right in.

Both approaches are wrong. The first causes problems, because you can't get into the trenches from afar. The second results in getting too deep into the trenches all at once, which can lead to drowning, because there are simply too many things to figure out simultaneously while burning through capital.

Our friend took a different approach. Leaving his job, where he was making in the mid six figures, he signed up to work the line at Chipotle, making minimum wage. Educating yourself, as our friend did, by getting into the trenches is a smart move, because it allows you to take the right amount of risk. Often aspiring entrepreneurs get caught up in risk-taking motivational jargon and take wild chances. There's no doubt that being an entrepreneur is one of the riskiest things you can do, but successful entrepreneurs are actually risk minimizers. That's what getting into the trenches allows you to do.

Our friend took the personal and emotional risk of leaving a cushy job and landed in a perfect spot to *learn*. He took detailed notes on everything he observed, from lean operations to staffing and training. He paid attention to where there was waste and where he could improve the customer experience.

From the trenches, he had an important insight: there are simply too many opportunities for breakdown in the restaurant industry. In a restaurant, "you have to earn your customers' business every single meal," he said. "If you mess up once, even if it's after someone has had a good experience ten times, the customer is likely gone, if not forever, for at least a few months." Previously he'd read that restaurants have an 85 percent attrition rate. But as many confident former bankers might, he figured that he could do better by managing tighter and making the numbers work. By jumping into the assembly line of an existing operation, he saw firsthand the challenging dynamics of a well-branded operation and realized that his time, energy, and capital would be better spent on a different idea. He's since gone on to start a successful financial technology business with very favorable margins and high customer retention.

The Farmers' Market Test

Ever been to a farmers' market and seen people selling a small amount of goods? They have a folding table, inventory that can fit in their car, and maybe one person helping them. They're running a lean operation. We advocate applying this approach to your idea before you go into full-scale launch mode. Test a version of your product or service with a select group of consumers. We've seen a number of products start this way and become national brands, including Health-Ade Kombucha, which we spotted at the Bel Air Farmers' Market more than five years ago. If you have an app, do as the online payments business Stripe did in its early days: don't just offer people a link to download your program, offer to install it for them. This is not a long-term scalable solution, but do whatever you can to get in front of consumers. Here are some factors to consider:

- What's the "homemade" version of your product?
- Where can you talk to fifty customers in a row about your product or service?
- How can you do this all in one day for no more than a few hundred dollars?

Treat every interaction as a learning opportunity. Pay attention to every word, every facial expression, and how long the other person stays. You're in the trenches: get all the info you can.

GET INTO THE TRENCHES WITH PURPOSE

Hopefully we've convinced you that it's worth getting as much first-hand experience as possible before beginning. To make the most of it, create a game plan in advance. We propose the following:

- Take a piece of paper, divide it into four quadrants, as shown in the chart on the next page, and fill in your answers.

WHAT DO I KNOW ALREADY ABOUT THIS IDEA?	WHAT DO I THINK I KNOW THAT I NEED TO CONFIRM?
WHAT DO I NEED TO LEARN?	WHAT AM I SO SURE OF THAT I JUST NEED TO START?

Then use your framework to create a plan to test your assumptions systematically and find answers to the things you don't know.

- Take note of all the customer touch points. Where, who, how, when are people consuming what you're offering? Dig into the experience, and understand each moment; this will help you iterate your offering.

- Support trench experience with desk research. Before you get in front of customers, what can you learn from others who have tried what you're trying? When businesses have failed in your space, what caused the failure? Was it unit economics, too much overhead, too much complexity? Then get into the trenches and pay particular attention to how you can solve those challenges.

IT BOILS DOWN TO FINDING THE RIGHT INSIGHT

Fundamentally, what you are doing in the trenches is looking for key insights. We always tell people that when we look at any business that was crazy successful, it stemmed from a single meaningful insight. It's an "aha" moment that is less than obvious but makes a ton of sense when you hear it. The deeper and better your insight, the better your business will be. Often an insight is something fundamental about a group of people's proclivities, desires, or pain points. Howard Schultz's insight was that Americans were craving a "third place" between work and home where they could have a sense of community and meet for conversation, like the Italian café. That was the seed of Starbucks. Larry Page and Sergey Brin had an insight about the way people search for information—the most common searches and most often chosen answers being considered the most accurate—leading to Google. We saw friends mixing vodka with Gatorade and realized that people were looking for a healthy component to their drinking experience. By no means are we insinuating that our insight was on a par with those of Larry Page and Howard Schultz—just that it can take multiple forms!

How to Look for Insights

There are patterns to look for to generate insights. Typically, they fall into one or more of the following categories:

- *New behaviors.* What are people, particularly early adopters, trying, tasting, liking, and buying for the first time? Can you spot the waves forming?
- *Life hacks and MacGyver fixes.* Ever used a paper clip as a collar stay? That's an example of a small hack—a creative solution in the moment. Where are people using these "duct tape"–type solutions in their lives? Can you provide what they're looking for?
- *Resources that were once abundant but now are scarce.* Capitalism can be wasteful when it comes to abundant resources. Inherently, valuable goods are treated as precious and less expensive goods are tossed to the side. But the value of things can change and often does. Can you notice any process in which there's a by-product that could be made more valuable than it is now?

Consider the guy who "invented" baby carrots. In the mid-1980s, Mike Yurosek became tired of throwing away four hundred tons of carrots a day in his Bakersfield, California, processing plant. They were too bent or broken to sell, so he first used them to feed his pigs. When their fat turned orange from eating so many, he decided to see if he could sell the discards somehow. At first, he shaped them by hand with a potato peeler. Then he bought an industrial green bean cutter, which happened to cut carrots into two-inch-long pieces. And voilà, baby carrots—and a whole new industry—were born. Mike's insight was partially inspired by his desire to avoid food waste, as well as by his ability to break the conventional belief that people wanted carrots of only a certain size. What started with an issue in the trenches became a learning experience, which led to a bankable business for an innovative product subcategory, one that many other companies would later enter. None of that would have come to pass if Mike hadn't been in the trenches, thinking about what he was observing. *Whereas many people focus on seeking information, successful people seek insights.*

THE TRENCHES ARE NOT JUST FOR BEFORE YOU LAUNCH

The concept of getting into the trenches doesn't apply just to those who are working toward launching. It can be as powerful when you are trying to pivot or to improve your offering.

One great example of finding your key insight while the business is running is the story of Darius Bikoff, the founder of Energy Brands and creator of Vitaminwater, whom Courtney got to work with at Goldman Sachs. He had a novel idea that would revolutionize the beverage space: People drank water and took vitamins, but what if you combined the two? His key insight that really helped the brand take off was actually a merchandising play he conceived after visiting many bodegas in New York City.

Although bodegas are small, they are pivotal to the sale of consumer products in New York City because there are few chain stores. Thus they are incredible for shelf presence because they are small and products stand out. During his visits, Bikoff realized that Vitaminwater was being shelved next to Gatorade, essentially blending in with a host of better-established colored liquids. "No," he thought, "this is water with vitamins.

It should be shelved in the water section." He convinced store owners to place his product in the water section, where, as colored water, it really "popped" off the shelf. He realized that, when placed next to water, Vitaminwater appealed to our instinctual love of bright colors. It was an exciting alternative, whereas when it stood next to Gatorade, it was fighting an uphill battle as an unknown brand. That insight enabled sales to really take off, and in 2007, he sold Energy Brands to Coca-Cola for $4.2 billion.

As Darius found out while driving around New York City, there's no substitute for getting deep into the trenches. If he hadn't been delivering the cases himself, he wouldn't have had his placement insight, and his brand might have failed! Even if you don't find a killer insight in the trenches, what you learn will be invaluable to creating success. Here are some of the insights we got while driving around the United States when we launched VEEV.

Pitching: From Telling Your Story to Selling Your Product

Watching bartenders explain VEEV to patrons could either be a nails-on-the-chalkboard or music-to-our-ears experience. Some bartenders compared the product to flavored vodka, and others called it an açaí liqueur. The different stories led to staggering sales differences. When a bartender likened VEEV to an açaí liqueur, people compared it to the sugary low-proof stuff their grandmothers drank and sales were low. When bartenders pitched it as a vodka alternative, sales were nearly ten times as good. That slight adjustment to the story made a huge impact on the top line. Imagine not noticing this staggering difference in sales conversion until five years down the line, when we were in all fifty states. We would have been in bad shape had we not been on barstools frequently! Being in the trenches early allowed us to see that happening and develop tighter processes to control how we were pitched. Small insight, major results.

Use Cases: Understand How People Consume Your Product

We also paid attention to how people mixed VEEV on their own. What we saw was that the mixer of choice was club soda or water with a squeeze of lemon or lime—low-calorie, low-sugar choices. That was a validating insight about how our consumers thought about our product. The perception was that we were the healthy alternative in the space, so we doubled down on that messaging. We made our signature drinks clean, with very few ingredients and low sugar content, and created the slogan "A better way to drink." Instead of building our marketing on how we wanted customers to drink our product, we let them dictate their preferences and built our marketing around that. It doesn't work this way for every product, but it did for ours, and there is a reason that "the customer is always right."

Distribution: Put Your Product in Danger of Being Purchased

Distributors have a tough job: there are too many products and not enough time to understand and sell each one adequately. Britt West and Raul Marmol of Plus Consulting, our first partners and advisers in the spirits industry, made that point crystal clear from day 1. That realization helped us understand that we had to be on top of our distributors and inspect what we expect. We learned that no one was going to push our product harder than we were, even if it was the distributor's job to do so. Furthermore, distribution doesn't stop after the sale. We can't tell you how many times we went into a restaurant or grocery store that had supposedly bought our product, only to find it nowhere to be seen. Getting the product on the shelf was the next battle, oftentimes with different gatekeepers. But you can fight only if you're in the trenches. More than once, we had a buyer say, "Sorry, but the product didn't sell," to which we answered, "That's correct, but it's because it never made it onto the shelf, so let's see what happens when it does." Usually the buyers were reasonable, but progress started with our being our own advocates.

Competition: Protect Your Product

A major realization that we had with VEEV was that bartenders don't always pour what a customer orders. This can happen for a variety of reasons: they're busy and don't have time to go get another bottle of your product, they simply don't care, something else is cheaper, or they're being incentivized by another company. Importantly, bartenders pouring someone else's brand or another group counterfeiting your product creates a double hit: the loss of revenue from a location not going through your inventory and, even more damaging, the potential loss of consumer trust among customers who associate your brand with an inferior product experience. Some innovative companies are solving just this problem, such as Jenda Technology, a company that helps customers and businesses defend against counterfeits through product authentication.

Whether consumers receive the wrong product purposefully or accidentally, seeing it occur changed the way we managed our business. We came to learn that bartenders were essential to our success as a brand, so we made a concerted effort to develop a relationship with every bartender we came into contact with. It was not easy, but it was key to our agenda, as bartenders were the gatekeepers of our industry. So we made sure to have "butts on barstools"—in other words, VEEV employees (including ourselves) in bars. Though we had not originally intended to spend time in bars, we needed to ensure that VEEV was moving and found it to be an important way to do so.

Overall, our trench experiences taught us to constantly check back in and never let ourselves, as founders, get too removed from customers. As our dad repeatedly said, "The devil is in the details," and boy, was he right—there's no substitute for experiencing your product or service the same way customers do.

THE POWER OF EARLY INSIGHTS

One important reason you want to get into the trenches as early as possible is that you want to discover your insights as soon as you can. Here's why: the smallest adjustment based on early insights can make massive differences over time. It's like flying an airplane: if you are flying from JFK to LAX and adjust your airplane's trajectory wrong by only one degree at takeoff, you'll end up landing fifty miles out into the Pacific Ocean.

Consider the story of the founders of Twitch.tv, now the world's leading video platform for gamers. Justin Kan's first company, Kiko Software, was a digital calendar, similar to Google's. When Kan and other founders realized that their calendar wasn't going to be a major success story, they decided to auction their page site on eBay, receiving $250,000. Subsequently, Kan and his business partner Emmett Shear used the money from the sale to launch Justin.tv, a site that would livestream people's lives, what they called "lifecasting." Though responses were mixed, many users began to request the ability to create their own online video streams. At the same time, the practice of streaming video games was popular but technologically difficult. By watching customer behavior, following market trends, and listening to customers, Kan and Shear realized that there was a major opportunity with gamers. They took that learning and spun off Twitch.tv, ultimately selling it to Amazon for nearly a billion dollars. The key here is that the founders weren't blinded by love for their original idea, which so often happens. Instead, they saw an insight early enough and changed course to a much more successful idea.

Another example of the power of finding insights early is a company called Aflore, a Colombian financial services platform launched by a company builder called Polymath Ventures. When Polymath was searching for how to assess the creditworthiness of an underserved population, the majority of whom didn't have a credit history, it became clear that numerous people in Latin America borrow from other people within their communities. How do those community lenders decide whom to lend to? They usually know the person personally and therefore can estimate their creditworthiness. That insight led to a whole new business model. Aflore engaged those community lenders as informal advisers to help it not only assess creditworthiness but become its primary distribution channel, making Aflore one of the first direct-sales lending companies in the world.

We love this example for a few reasons. First, this insight is something that the founders of Aflore couldn't have discovered through desk research. They discovered it by conducting in-depth interviews with a wide range of people about their borrowing and lending behaviors and then creatively synthesizing the information they gathered.

Second, it's a reminder of how innovation stems from insights, and insights result from observing human behavior. Pay attention to what people are doing or trying to do most naturally, and you will uncover insights. Notice that we used the word "uncover." That's because insights are found, not created. You need to be out there talking to people, seeking to understand what they are doing and why, rather than in a room brainstorming.

Make sure you personally are getting in front of customers and asking questions to understand their experience, rather than just using focus groups. Incentivize your employees to identify insights as well. Your sales team may be best suited to discover insights, whereas your engineering team may be the one that needs to hear them. Be sure there are clear lines of communication between those teams—eating together can be a great tool to help them share!

Are You the Next Steve Jobs?

Steve Jobs once said, "A lot of times, people don't know what they want until you show it to them." One could even argue that Henry Ford was saying the same thing when he remarked, "If I had asked people what they wanted, they would have said faster horses," in reference to creating the Ford Model T car at the turn of the twentieth century. Truly visionary CEOs are like that; their job is *not* to listen to anyone and to create a whole new future. But the Steve Jobses of the world are extremely rare. Chances are that, like us, you're not one of them. This means your job is to get into places where you can listen to potential customers and pay close attention to what you are hearing and seeing.

GET INTO THE TRENCHES ON PRICING

When you're starting out with a consumer product, it's tempting to do research on standard margins for your industry and then to price based on those margins. But because you're producing small quantities and have high unit costs, margin pricing causes you to price your product too high. Remember, you're introducing something new into the marketplace that no one knows about, and you need to get buyers. Don't fool yourself that you've created such a wonderful product or service that price will be no object. You need to price according to what consumers would expect to pay for something comparable. Initially you'll make less per unit, but broad sales are important when you are starting off. You're trying to win loyal customers who will market for you via social media and spread awareness by word of mouth to build your brand.

We call this "product self-awareness." You need to be aware of where you are in your development cycle to know what price to charge. You cultivate this awareness by having a deep understanding of your customers' psyche, which comes from listening to lots of them. We think that Hylete, a premium performance apparel company, did a great job of this. It originally tested its product quality, fit, and pricing with the CrossFit community before broadening out to the athleisure and functional fitness markets.

Getting the price right really matters—and you should be working on it *before* you develop your product. That way you can pull the plug if you discover that people aren't willing to pay enough for what you want to create.

Tech products and services have an analogous problem. As with consumer products, it's not about getting the best margin at the start but finding people who will pay for what you have because they see value in it. Beware of going too low. Especially with hardware, don't underprice it, because companies tend to value what they pay for, and if they get a bargain, they might fail to use it.

Though many elements of the startup world continue to change, the fundamentals of pricing remain the same: in order to run a sustainable business, your price must be higher than your costs but not so high that consumers turn to alternatives for your goods or services.

Questions You Should Be Asking

When you get your product or service in front of people, you should be surveying them on a wide number of questions. To give you a leg up on consumer surveying, here's a site for the questionnaire we sometimes have consumers fill out regarding products: Shortcutyourstartup.com.

Though this may seem intuitive, pricing has actually become a more complex topic for startups. Consumers in today's world have fast and reliable access to information and therefore can make more informed purchase decisions. This happens across the board, from brick-and-mortar retail pricing to e-commerce. Think about it—have you ever been in a store, let's say Whole Foods Market, looking for a product and checked Amazon on your phone to ensure that you weren't being charged more for your protein bars in the store? (Perhaps a more relevant activity before Amazon acquired Whole Foods!) Or maybe you have been on Amazon looking for a toothbrush and then checked another website such as Jet.com to ensure that Amazon's price was reasonable. Consumers today know if your product is priced higher than the competition's and are interested in getting a good deal. Therefore, developing a reputation for inconsistent or "targeted" pricing won't help your company with sales or branding.

Similarly, because of the next-day-shipping phenomenon, your pricing really has to be reflective of product value rather than factors such as location or convenience. As price is increasingly tied to product value, startups have begun to balance a number of factors that help create the perception of product value, including emotion, sustainability, and transparency. Everlane, the online apparel company that both designs and produces all of its goods, is pushing the boundaries of transparent and emotional pricing by implementing a "fully transparent" pricing structure. It not only breaks down the price of each item on its site and

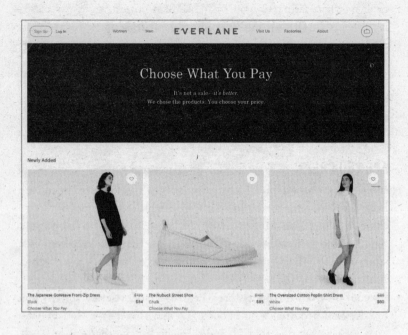

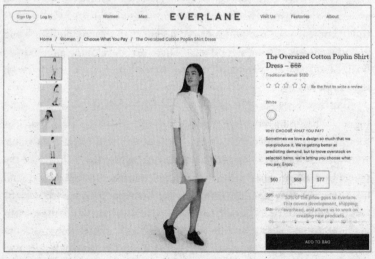

explains where the money goes (manufacturing, overhead, etc.) but also, in some instances, allows its customers to set their own prices through a "choose what you pay" promotion.

Though it may seem crazy, this sort of transparency has led to a positive flurry of PR and incremental sales. Consumers feel comfortable shopping with Everlane, because they know where their money is going, understand the value they are receiving, and feel empowered.

ARE YOU CREATING A PRODUCT OR BUILDING A COMPANY (OR BOTH)?

Not all ideas can turn into full-fledged companies. For instance, there was a team on our TV show that created a shish kabob flipper for grilling. It was a great gadget, and the team could probably make a few million dollars with it. But it's likely never going to become a $100 million company.

Why does this matter? Because you need to be crystal clear about what you have and build to that. Building a company rather than just a product affects your funding, your hiring, your infrastructure, and every other decision you make. Companies are able to share learning across products, which typically leads to better and better products and stock-keeping units (SKUs). It also affects your cost structure. Producing only one product makes your fixed costs particularly onerous, as they're being amortized across only one item. Building a company means sharing fixed costs among products and developing some economies of scale.

Too often, we see entrepreneurs who incorrectly think they have the next $100 million company and make choices that end up in failure. They try to sell themselves to funders as the next $100 million company, which just feels unrealistic, or they do raise capital successfully, taking on far too much capital over multiple funding rounds and diluting all investors—including themselves—at each consecutive raise. Remember, the more you raise, the bigger your exit has to be for it to be worthwhile. It's okay to say, "I'm going to build a business that does $5 million in sales," and figure out how to do it sustainably and profitably. Know what you're trying to do before you set out to do it.

Use available sales information to help you get a sense of your idea's potential. If you're the shish kabob flipper creator, for instance, check out what the most successful products like this sold on *Shark Tank* and marketed *As Seen on TV* are. Find out what success looks like based on units sold, margins, top line. How and where are the products typically sold?

We know this sounds really obvious, but make sure you have a realistic idea of what you can sell before you place that first order. A startup coach has told us many horror stories of people who spent every dime they had to purchase 10,000 units of their great idea that are now gathering dust in their garages.

TURNING A PRODUCT INTO A COMPANY

One way to think about whether you can create a company from your idea is to focus on its feature or benefit and see if you can extend that. Let's stick with the kabob flipper. That's a feature: it helps you flip your kabob. What's the benefit of it? It makes grilling easier and makes grilled food turn out tastier. Can you somehow use the technology you employed in the flipper to build a wide variety of products? That's how you go from a product to a company. You get into the door with the kabob flipper and then sell the "corn on the cob flipper" and the grill that's synched to your smartphone; then you've created a company. George Foreman epitomizes a business that used one product—the George Foreman grill—to start an entire company.

The same thinking works for an app. What's your special feature? What benefit does it offer? Can that be extended?

Headspace is another great example of a company that started as a simple service in a space loaded with apps and turned into a viable company. It took a simple meditation product and transformed it into a successful startup that has raised nearly $40 million. We were so impressed by the company that we invested in it. Though it originally offered general meditation services for free, it now offers five areas of services: foundation, health, performance, relationships, and Headspace Pro (less guidance during the meditation), and generates revenue by selling subscriptions to its services. Headspace encourages new customers to try its service through a ten-day free trial. If consumers love the product and want to access a broader selection of content, they can select one of four payment plans: monthly, yearly, every two years, or lifetime.

We struggled with the product-versus-company issue ourselves with VEEV. In hindsight, we didn't transition from one to the other fast enough. We tried to move from the core VEEV product to the "better way to drink" spirits company with our organic, ready-to-drink cocktail brand extension, VitaFrute. But we probably took eighteen months too long to launch it. We spent nine months developing VitaFrute and another few months launching it, time that we could have compressed if we'd thought it out better in advance.

One of our biggest lessons from that experience was to be sure to think about your product road map early because it will impact the way you build your infrastructure. We should have had the extension concept ready and waiting so we didn't lose momentum.

There's a tricky balance here when you're first starting out. You don't want to get too far ahead of yourself, thinking that you are the next big grilling company when you've got one kabob flipper. But if you do want to create that bigger play, you need to be also thinking about it.

We advise that entrepreneurs create their product road map starting from day one, whether they're talking to investors or bootstrapping it themselves, even though they're not going to execute the whole road map at the start. That way, if the shish kabob flipper is successful, you're ready with where you want to go next; you won't have time to make that decision when you're already there. Don't let the wave go past you because you didn't start paddling soon enough or hard enough.

YOUR HERO PRODUCT

When starting out, everyone needs a hero product. It's that special item or service that creates buzz, the standout upon which you build your brand and company. It gets folks to your website or motivates them to pick your item off the shelf, and it keeps them coming back for more. Your hero product also helps pull in your core customer, the main driver of your business.

Why does the hero product matter? Depending on what you're selling, it can help with one or more of the following.

- **Word of mouth.** The hero product helps you go viral. For restaurants, for instance, it could be the one thing on the menu that gets people buzzing and blogging, such as the cronut (a croissant-doughnut pastry invented in New York City).
- **Door opener.** It gets people to try you out. You see this often in companies with premium models such as Headspace and Spotify that offer free or basic plans to get people in the door and then have more expensive options to choose from once they've tried them.
- **Cost controller.** A hero product should be the core of all your products and create volume, which gives you economies of scale in production and expands your margins enough to cover your costs. The same applies to a core service: it's not just about what the product is but about how you can spread the production or offering costs across as many SKUs as possible with limited incremental costs. Think color extensions, for instance. They require virtually no change to the product but provide appeal to different potential buyers that increases sales.

Often, first-time entrepreneurs don't understand the need for anchoring their product line on the hero. We see this a lot with the *Hatched* competitors. One company had seventy-two different SKUs, with nothing as the standout. In addition to the enormous overhead of creating and packaging all those products, it's confusing to consumers: What do you want me to buy? The old adage "trying to be all things to all people" comes to mind. It results in ineffective marketing, because you're spreading your efforts too wide.

On the flip side, there are smart companies such as Pop & Suki, which makes handbags and a suite of other accessories. It started with one customizable camera bag that was unique and felt special due to the customization. It gifted this hero product to influencers and celebrities, who began talking about it before the company took off. That opened doors with consumers, and now the company is expanding into a host of other cool SKUs.

Offering too many products or services from the start comes from not knowing who your customers are and what they really want. Those lessons are exactly what you should walk out of the trenches with. Although it's tempting to try to appeal to everyone, you need to focus your time, funding, and effort on what the branding expert Julie Supan called the high-expectation customer (HXC). An HXC is your ideal user, "the most discerning person within your target demographic."

If you leave the trenches without an idea of who your HXCs are or how to appeal to them, your company will have trouble growing, as you will be missing a key piece of the equation: a loyal and dedicated customer base. Therefore, beyond learning about who they are and what they want, strive to appeal to and delight them. They are most likely the customers who will drive your sales from the beginning.

Finding Your Hero Product

- **What's the staple that will get the most people in the door as soon as possible, as Headspace's basic plan does?**
- **What's the frequency of purchasing? How can it be like selling diapers rather than diamonds?**
- **What's the main reason that drives your customers to purchase your product?**
- **Who do you *want* your customers to be? That is, do you want to sell to the HR director of a company or to the CEO? We can tell you who has more decision-making power.**
- **What's the most press-worthy idea, with a story that's easy to tell?**

Know if You're a Speedboat or a Sailboat: Business Strategy

There's a saying that a successful businessperson has to have a microscope on one eye and a telescope on the other. If the last Switchup was about investigating as many details as possible in advance—the microscope—this one is the telescope, looking at the big picture to understand what kind of company you need to create to succeed. Fundamentally, it's about taking your best guess on the right business strategy for your business at the start.

We like to think about it using a boat analogy. Because of the forces of globalization, innovation, and technology, businesses such as local hardware stores and bookstores are harder and harder to keep afloat in today's market. Millions of such businesses are floating around in a sea of commerce without a specific direction, like dinghies. Consumers can find more and more of whatever they are looking for from businesses such as Amazon and Alibaba—the massive cargo ships of the sea that are disrupting everyone in their wakes. A dinghy won't cut it anymore; you need a bigger boat to win the race these days.

As the title of this Switchup suggests, we think you need to be either a speedboat or a sailboat. Figuring out what kind of boat you're launching is critical, because it will determine many key decisions, especially fund-raising. In this Switchup, we explain the difference between a speedboat strategy and a sailboat strategy and how timing will affect your choice. We'll help you determine how to win the race with a speedboat and what you need to do to catch the wind as a sailboat— because chances are that's the boat you should be piloting. We also put on our VC hats and walk you through the basics of funding rounds and valuation so you can pay for the boat you've chosen.

SPEEDBOAT VERSUS SAILBOAT

If you're a speedboat, you're the first mover. You know where you're heading and are trying to create and dominate a whole new category. Speedboats require a lot of fuel and often run unprofitably (and therefore unsustainably) to become market leaders, because they must end up as number one or two at the finish line. This is due primarily to what's called *network effects*. The term refers to the fact that in such businesses, each incremental user makes the service more valuable, increasing "stickiness" for existing users and making it easier to acquire the next customer. Lyft/Uber, Airbnb, ClassPass, and Facebook are familiar examples of this winner-take-most phenomenon fueled by network effects. The more people use them versus a competitor, the more likely they are to be used by the next customer.

The Stickier, the Better

"Stickiness" is a term used to describe how difficult it is for a customer to switch to a competitor. Think phone contracts, for instance. You can increase stickiness through contracts and terms or by increasing the value of your product or service. We like sticky businesses because, by definition, it's hard to leave them.

If you are a speedboat, you must be first or second. One of the ways we came up with this Switchup was by experience: we invested in what, in hindsight, had to be speedboats to be successful and weren't—and they didn't make it. Companies that fall into this category are Uber competitors such as Wheelz, which, because of the network effects of car- and ride-sharing, needed to achieve scale as fast as possible to start benefiting from network effects but didn't do so fast enough. That's the risky thing about speedboats: there's a window of time in which they have to get to the top, and if they can't reach scale before they run out of cash, they're stuck in the middle of the ocean with no fuel.

Sailboat companies, on the other hand, are heading in a general direction, but are beholden to the winds. Sailboats pay attention to where things are moving, leaving options open. Typically they're not going to get there first, but they spend time learning from first movers and understanding unmet customer needs. In some cases, they might even be waiting for trends to catch up to them.

A subset of a sailboat is what Carter likes to call "hanging-around-the-rim" companies. These are startups that grow as a by-product of a speedboat. For instance, think about the many businesses that have developed as a by-product of Airbnb's success: property managers, rental insurance, cleaning services, scheduling apps. The demand for those services greatly increased—seemingly out of nowhere—as soon as Airbnb hit critical mass.

One of the more successful of the hanging-around-the-rim companies created in the wake of Airbnb is Pillow. It's a vacation rental company that specializes in property management for short-term rentals, handling aspects of hosting from marketing to communicating with guests, booking, pricing, and cleaning. Pillow charges hosts 15 percent of their booking fees to use the service so that hosts can list on Airbnb without having to do the work and customers get a high-quality experience. By merging online and real-world operations, this symbiotic relationship serves Airbnb as well: more and better listings mean more customers and, better yet, more happy customers.

A hanging-around-the-rim company that took a different approach to Airbnb's success is the ALICE app, a software company that joins the various departments of hotels on a single operations platform, connecting hotel guests and staff. ALICE increases efficiency across the hotel industry while reducing costs and enhancing customer experience, two crucial factors in hotels' profitability in the wake of the competitive forces created by Airbnb. Both Pillow and ALICE were sailboats out in the water that pounced on opportunities in the wake of a larger boat. ALICE has raised more than $13 million since its founding in 2012, and Pillow has raised more than $2.5 million since 2014.

Sailboats can be just as successful as speedboats. The messaging app Slack is a great example. Its founders were originally working as a company called Tiny Speck, helping to create Glitch, a short-lived browser-based MMO (massively multiplayer online) game that launched in 2009 and stopped operations in 2012. Glitch provided users with a world where players could interact, collect resources, trade, and personalize their characters. Although Stewart Butterfield, Glitch's founder, had leftover VC funding when Glitch failed and could have paid back that sum of money to his investors, he realized that his Glitch team had created fun and engaging ways to encourage people to perform work tasks and that he was sitting on a robust, customized communication platform. He and his team quickly pivoted in January 2013; by June, they were beta-testing the Slack platform.

Slack is the perfect sailboat story because they already had a company, funding, and engineers when Butterfield had his insight and so were able to take advantage of the trend toward messaging as a standard of communication faster than anyone else. If a new business was to have seen the same trend and tried to compete, it would have spent a year finding talent and funding, a year during which Slack was going full steam ahead. Today Slack, currently valued at more than $5 billion, is creating the market as much as the product. In fact, it is quite likely that Slack powers intracompany messaging at the very place where you work.

Catching a trend at the right time is a game changer, and the ability to do so is what separates the Slack founders from others who have drowned in Slack's wake. As we have said, with the power of social media and global interconnectivity, trends emerge and accelerate so quickly nowadays. As with Slack, there can be a real advantage to being a sailboat where you are in the game, with enough money and a team built up, not burning through all your cash, so that when you spot a new trend, you can really take off.

LET'S TALK STRATEGY

As we said earlier, when we talk speedboat versus sailboat, we're talking about making a choice regarding your core business strategy. Far too many entrepreneurs lack a guiding strategy or confuse strategy with tactics. Strategy has a higher purpose: it has the end goal in mind and then uses tactics to get to the end goal. Strategy must come before tactics. You have to decide how to win in the general sense before you start to come up with specific actions. As the business guru Michael Porter famously said, "The essence of strategy is choosing what not to do."

We can't say it strongly enough: don't set out in your boat until you're clear which boat you're taking. Yes, your strategy will likely change as you go on, but you'll definitely flail, wasting precious time and money and therefore momentum and competitive advantage, if you skip this step.

Determining if you're a speedboat or a sailboat—and when to switch boats, if at all—is a key to success. Take the food and hospitality genius Danny Meyer, for example. For years, he created some of the highest-end fine dining experiences in one of the food capitals of the world, New York City. His restaurant Eleven Madison Park is one of only six to receive three Michelin stars in the entire city. Typically, high-end restaurants aren't about speed to market. It's a sailboat business model that, by definition, doesn't scale.

At the same time, however, Meyer was also operating a small food cart in Madison Square Park in New York City. As the cart gained popularity, he opened a more permanent installation—a "shack" with no inside seating. That one shack kept sailing along profitably for nearly ten years, and enlarged the menu offering into hamburgers, fries, and shakes. At the same time that Meyer's Shake Shack was expanding its menu, the economy took a downturn, and the "better-burger" move-

ment began to take off. Meyer's 100 percent Angus beef, hormone- and
antibiotic-free burgers had a major opportunity to expand outside of
just one park in New York. As a result of the economic climate, residents
of major urban cities wanted to continue to go out to upscale meals, but
not necessarily as frequently or at expensive restaurants. Meyer realized that Shake Shack had a major market opportunity, and he took his
speedboat moment. He raised serious money and began opening Shake
Shacks like crazy, grabbing market share in the better-burger space. The
chart below shows how fast the company grew, after being stable for
many years. Ultimately it IPO'd for $1.3 billion.

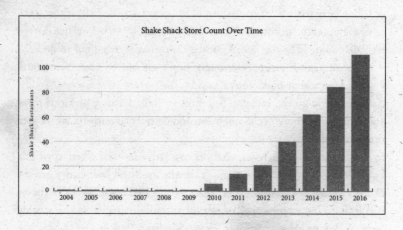

Speedboat or sailboat, there are dangers in the water no matter your
strategic choice. The rewards of being a successful speedboat are huge,
but the likelihood of success is slim. Most nontech companies cannot
scale quickly enough, and even some that can are not able to do so with
sustainable unit economics. Take Homejoy, a housecleaning company
that had trouble with customer retention. It was going for a land grab
when it launched, charging more than $85 for 2.5-hour housecleanings,
but it ran out of steam when many customers used its $20 promotion
and never reused the service. Homejoy had no backup plan, no sail, so
there was only one way its story could end.

A sailboat strategy isn't always perfect either. There's typically a bunch of competitors sailing around in the water with you, because they've seen the same thing as you, and therefore you have less room for error. If you don't catch the wind of an opportunity, it's likely that another boat will.

PICKING YOUR VESSEL

When deciding on your strategy, start with these questions:

- Are you racing to acquire customers as fast as possible in a winner-take-all market? Or are you selling an interim product or service until you discover your hero product?
- Are you trying to be first to market, or is there already a pioneer?
- Are you seeing some opportunity in what a speedboat is creating that you have some time to develop?

Your answers to these questions will help your decision-making process, but there are other factors to consider as well. The upside of being an early mover is that you are not set to industry standards, may receive brand-building press, and can more easily develop economies of scale because you have the greatest volume of customers by virtue of being first. But being a first mover is not just expensive but also challenging. You're often required to educate consumers and in some cases introduce new behaviors before you can really sell. Often, first movers are like older siblings, learning the hard lessons while paving the way for the next in line to come in and make hay.

In certain businesses, though, such as those with expensive supply chains or strong network effects, being a first or at least an early mover provides a huge advantage. Think about a business with an expensive manufacturing process, such as an auto manufacturer. There's a reason there were only a few dominant players in the US automotive market for over a century, until Tesla came along: the barriers to entry are massive. Once a full-scale manufacturing base is set up, it's very hard for others to undercut you from a pricing standpoint without losing huge sums of money. As a newcomer, you will not likely be able to get the economies of scale the earlier player now has, and either your prices or margins will suffer.

Similarly, in businesses with significant network effects, such as Uber, Airbnb, and Facebook, it's very difficult to compete as a late entrant. The Facebook user experience comes down to connecting with other people in the social network, so it improves with each new user. With more than 1 billion users, Facebook is now so dominant that it would be tough to beat it at its own game now.

Some additional questions to consider when determining whether you are a speedboat or a sailboat:

1. How much capital can you access, and at what cost?

Can you actually raise the funds you need to be a speedboat? You might be able to raise $100 million, but only if you give up 90 percent of the company to outside investors. Will all the blood, sweat, and tears be worth the potential payout?

2. How fast can you get to a market leadership position?

No surprises here, but if you're building a speedboat, speed matters. Are there others in the marketplace that are better positioned to get to the top faster than you, regardless of how much capital you can access? You should be really doing your due diligence here to know the competitive landscape.

3. How fully baked does your product or service need to be to get to the top?

If you want to be a speedboat, don't overcook your product. Nail your HXC, as mentioned in the last chapter, and then focus on finding the features that make 80 percent of the market happy. Don't waste time trying to improve the experience of the last 20 percent. That said, be conscious of which customers you're paying attention to. More on this in later chapters, when we talk about serving the *right* customers.

4. What will make you go viral?

Businesses don't go viral on their own; they need entrepreneurs to light the fire. If you need to move fast, you must find ways to have every stakeholder spread the word on your behalf. Two businesses we invested in did that really well. Thrive Market, a health and wellness e-tailer (think Whole Foods meets Costco online), built an excellent affiliate program through which it incentivized influencers to promote its products to their respective audiences. By developing those relationships and promoting those influencers through paid social media, Thrive was able to develop a win-win relationship with its affiliates. Thrive was successfully developing a group of dedicated brand evangelists, while the affiliates were being boosted by Thrive's paid social media, increasing their followings. It was an uncommon strategy, as most brands would have simply offered 20 percent of sales to their affiliates. By spending its marketing dollars on encouraging paying influencers to post on social media, Thrive drove awareness and incentivized the influencers to want to post more content.

ClassPass, the leading fitness booking platform in the United States, took a different approach. It knew it needed to grow extremely fast because of the winner-take-all dynamics in the market. So it used the door-opener tactic we spoke of in the previous chapter and created an "unlimited" plan through which customers could pay one monthly fee and go to as many fitness classes in as many different venues as they liked, no exceptions. That was very expensive for ClassPass, and though the company generated less of a profit on those "superusers," the unlimited plan gained a significant amount of attention. ClassPass essentially used its pricing structure as a marketing tactic to fuel growth.

What that plan did was enable it to build a strong brand with high awareness and get a bunch of people in the door. Once it had saturated the market, it made a challenging but successful transition to "capped" plans, in which the classes each person could take per month were limited. In doing so, the company's founders made the business profitable. Had they done so off the bat, the experience would have been just like everyone else's, and who's to say who would have won?

5. How can technology help?

Technology, in general, is enabling more speedboats. The Honest Company is a great example. Historically, if you wanted to build a consumer brand, it was all about getting the buy-in of the big retailers. Target, Walmart, and the other big chains could make or break your business, because they were your path to customers. The Honest Company proved that to no longer be the case. It used technology to go direct to consumers and built an online brand for three years before starting to sell through retail channels.

Even with a sailboat, your chance to catch the wind is coming more quickly than ever before, because of technology. It's become so much easier to connect to your customers, so you should be getting faster to insights that can advise you what direction to move in. Ten years ago, with VEEV, our customer was distributors, and their customers were retailers. People would ask, "Who's buying your product?" and we really had no idea. We knew who was on our social media, but that wasn't the full picture by any means. Then, during the last eighteen months we owned VEEV, the technology came along to allow for real-time data. Using mobile-accessible coupons, first popular with Millennials, we could see who was buying, what the repeat purchase rates were, and which SKUs were being bought more often. No matter your strategy, one question you should constantly be asking yourself is "How can tech accelerate this?"

6. Is the timing right?

Your idea matters, PMF matters, funding matters, and your team matters (a lot). But none of those matters more than timing. If customers are demanding what you're creating, you can find the business model. Plenty of hugely successful companies have found their business/revenue model long after they started—think Facebook, for instance. If you can show traction or present a grand vision, you can attract capital and talent. But if your timing is off, it will all be for nothing. This is particularly true of a speedboat, where you have to hit the timing perfectly so that you don't run out of fuel.

Think about Airbnb: timing made all the difference. It started during the recession. Until then, especially when everyone was feeling "rich," how likely were you to let strangers rent your home or, more weirdly, a bedroom in your home? But during the recession, everyone could use some extra cash, and this was an easy way to get it.

Behind the timing issue is the fact that speedboat companies condition consumer behavior. They do something that at the beginning seems weird, but soon it seems ordinary and sparks similar behavior across totally different industries. Now not only do millions of people rent Airbnb properties instead of hotels, but the concept of sharing has conditioned us to think about ownerships differently. For example, many Millennials are asking "Why should I own a lawn mower? I'll just rent one when I need it." Or "Why should my lawn mower just sit in my garage? I'll rent it out."

If you're thinking that the conditions aren't right for you for a speedboat business and are wondering about what a good idea to launch is, it's worth paying attention to up-and-coming speedboats. With tons of venture capital money behind them, speedboats are likely paying to educate your future customers. That's phenomenal if you can take advantage of it. Think about what behavior is being conditioned, such as having someone deliver anything you want to you wherever you are. What opportunities are companies creating for products or services that you might offer? How can you get into the game with your sails raised, ready for that big speedboat to open up a whole new industry?

For instance, Uber and Airbnb have shown that a well-thought-out rating system can create the trust needed for people to share intimate spaces. What can you do now that those companies have spent billions of dollars teaching people to trust? Pay attention to your best guess on which behaviors will stick—and which may not make sense in a few years.

Here's an example. One of Carter's favorite companies is a subscription food business called Daily Harvest. These days, there is a subscription box for seemingly everything, and many consumers have been conditioned to order some of the items they consume regularly via subscription. The nimble team at Daily Harvest combined the emerging distribution model with the growing consumer demand for healthy and convenient meals to launch a superfood subscription business. Daily Harvest delivers a suite of products—currently flash-frozen smoothies, soups, chia parfaits, and overnight oats—on a weekly basis to health-conscious consumers all over the United States. The recipes are put together by nutritionists and chefs, and the freezing method keeps in more flavor and nutrients than conventional methods do. This is a great example of excellent execution paired with the right timing.

It's all about timing. As of this writing, for instance, if you're creating a company in the cannabis industry, you're a little ahead. But if you wait until a year from now, you're probably going to be behind. The people who are going to succeed are those with their sail up, waiting for their speedboat moment. They're waiting to see what direction the laws are going to take. There are all sorts of businesses that can be created around this industry if conditions are right: cannabis food products, subscription service businesses, innovative new consumption methods such as inhalers, and more. So if this appeals to you, you want to adopt a sailboat strategy so you will be able to catch the wind when conditions are right.

HINT: YOU'RE PROBABLY A SAILBOAT

After thinking through the issues in the previous section, chances are you've concluded that you're a sailboat. Most of us start sailboat companies of one sort or another. That's because once you are a speedboat, you are less flexible, and there's often no going back. Therefore, the choice to be a speedboat is a much riskier one.

With a sailboat, because the wind is variable, you have to know when to push to take advantage of the gust and when you can bob around. Even if you fail to catch the gust, you are probably not out of the game.

Since sailboats succeed by catching the right wind at the right time, to be a successful sailor, you must pay extremely close attention to your surroundings and really understand context: What is happening and why? To do this well, you have to be able to:

- See beyond the here and now
- Identify trends
- Extrapolate how to get from here to there
- Be ready to move when the timing is right

See the sidebar below for our tips on increasing your ability to be in the right place at the right time.

Tips for Sailing to Success

- Know your industry intimately. Spend time finding out what other people are doing in your space so that you can capitalize on their insights to find your own.
- Look at data: what things are increasing and decreasing in your industry—sales trends, user behaviors, and so on?
- Focus on building brand loyalty now; it's too hard to build loyalty when you become a speedboat, because everything is happening so fast.
- Nurture the capital you have to increase your runway. Limit your fixed costs to maximize your flexibility and ability to pivot. This will allow you to sail longer without the pressure of constant fund-raising!
- Put processes into place to get new products to market quickly when it's time.

CATCHING TREND WINDS

Fundamentally, success as a sailboat comes down to trend spotting, and that isn't easy. We've invested in businesses too early, too late, and just in time. Here are some things to think about in order to capture the winds of change.

- **Industry.** What's starting to change at the industry level? What are you seeing all the competitors in a sector starting to do or stop doing?

- **Economics.** Where are we in the economic cycle, and how will that impact your idea? Are we coming out of a recession or at what feels like the top of the market? How are people's spending habits going to evolve over the next three years? How can you cater to those changes?
- **Government.** What new laws are being enacted that might create new opportunities? For instance, are there new laws governing drones or health care that you can take advantage of?
- **Technology.** Where are the biggest technological gains occurring? Where are they currently being applied, and, more important, where have they not been applied yet?
- **Media.** How are people consuming information? How are ideas spreading that are different and novel? Where are teenagers going for information?
- **Social.** What trends are emerging from the aging population and/or Millennials regarding lifestyle, food, clothing, and more?

Finally, what are the ripple effects of innovations that have already hit the market or are likely to hit the market in coming years? If (when?) driverless cars arrive, what will they impact? If they reduce car ownership and the need for parking because they are in constant circulation, what might we do with all those extra parking garages?

Brainstorm what factors might impact you, then do research on what's happening in those areas, and draw conclusions. Or do reading in those areas, and think about the implications. It's important to keep checking the wind. That's what strategy meetings, conferences, and conversations with those outside your field are for: they give you a chance to think more broadly and find connections between what you are doing and the wider world. That's the essence of trend spotting.

Even for big companies, it's not easy to get the timing on trends right. When the two of us met the head of West Coast e-commerce for Facebook, he talked about how Facebook had been slower to go mobile than it should have been. The company was focused on leading the next wave: video. That's why Facebook started buying all kinds of video companies, added the video icon, started showing videos in people's news feeds, and separated Facebook Messenger from Facebook, and why Mark Zuckerberg switched from saying "We're a mobile-first company" to "We're a video-first company." They wanted to have their own sailboat in place, even if it meant entering the video trend earlier than others.

Of course, companies as dominant as Facebook are not just following trends, they're setting them. That's why it makes sense for you to watch what the behemoths are doing and be the first to follow their lead. If Facebook is trying to be a video-first company, what could you be doing? Create the video content it's trying to promote, and you're going to get a bunch of free lift in the early days. Alternatively, if you're hanging around the Facebook rim, maybe you see a need for a platform to connect companies with filmmakers to make branded content. There are opportunities to think like this all over the place; just watch the waves!

THE "RINGS OF SATURN" ROLLOUT STRATEGY

Once you have created your business strategy, next up is your rollout strategy. How are people going to find out about your offering? Let's say you've invented an eco-friendly shower faucet. Do you launch it only in California because the people there are tree huggers? In Starwood Hotels because the company is eco-conscious and will promote it? Is there an activist or celebrity who embodies the message your brand stands for?

We think of a rollout strategy as being like a planet's rings. Where do you start to find your early adopters, the dedicated customers who make up your first and innermost ring? Who's going to lead to the most viral growth? After you acquire those customers, who's in the next ring? And the next?

With VEEV, our first ring was on-premises in Beverly Hills and Hollywood, which meant trendy bars, clubs, and restaurants. We would get into all these hot places, and then when someone asked, "Where can I buy it?" there were one or two liquor stores where it was available. Once we created some initial demand, we expanded to the next ring: liquor stores and other retail outlets in the same area. It wasn't until about the third year that we got into any chains, which took us national.

When a brand creates a waiting list, it's using a pull strategy. We created demand and then let people flock to it. Alternatively, when you're sampling a new food or drink at a Whole Foods, the company is employing a push strategy: If you put this into your mouth, we think you'll buy it! Push push.

Which is better? It depends on the industry, your product, and your style. The important thing is to be intentional about it and have a game plan. These days, to acquire customers, you most likely need to use both push and pull tactics, whether pushing free trials or using social media influencers to generate awareness and excitement. We do a deep dive on customer acquisition in Switchup 7.

FUNDING THE BOAT RIDE

Whether you're a speedboat or sailboat and no matter what your rollout strategy is, you need capital. Sometimes first-time entrepreneurs shy away from investors because they're confused about how investment funding works. This should not be your reason for not raising capital. So you can feel a bit more prepared to have the needed conversations, opposite is a chart of the rounds of investment that turn an idea into a company ready for an IPO: what each round typically raises, what types of investors get involved in each round, and factors VCs consider in each round before saying yes. We also offer tips for getting funded when you need to and the basics of equity and valuation. Be aware, however, that these are complex issues, so before venturing (pun intended) into this territory, we strongly encourage you to get advice from an experienced business attorney.

Venture Funnel: Typical Metrics

	PRE-SEED	SEED	SERIES A	SERIES B	SERIES C
Amount	$500k-$1m	$1m-$3m	$5m-$12m	$10m-$30m	$30m+
Valuation	$1m-$5m	$3m-$8m	$10m-$40m	$50m-$200m	$100m+
Investors	Friends & Family, Angels, Pre-Seed Funds	Angels, Micro VCs	VCs	VCs	VCs, PE
Team	Smart, committed guys/girls with relevant expertise/skills.		No "star" VPs yet. Often good director-level hires. Proven ability to attract & manage great people.	Senior leadership in most functions. Proven ability to recruit senior people.	Complete senior management team.
Product/Market Fit	Market research indicates strong need for the product. Prototype / very basic product with first activity.	Strong indications of Product/Market Fit from early customers/users. Initial liquidity on the platform.	Clear PMF and increasing evidence of PMF in larger market.		
Unit Economics	Unit economics should work based on intuitive theory.	Some evidence unit economics work.	Unit economics work and indicate that they will continue to work at scale.	Conviction unit economics work at scale or they work already.	Unit economics work.
Monthly Net Rev	-	<$50k	<$200k	$200k-$500k	$1m+
Expected Exit Multiple	25-50x	20-40x	10-15x	8-12x	5-7x

Great Pitch Decks

Here's a link to eighteen fund-raising decks from real startups, including BuzzFeed, LinkedIn, Foursquare, Airbnb: https://attach.io/startup-pitch-decks/. We encourage you to take a look to see in particular how they framed their early asks. In the average seed round, the amount raised was $1.1 million and the average number of investors per round was 4.7.

GETTING FUNDING WHEN YOU NEED IT

Having been on both sides of pitches for more than a decade, we have strong opinions on how to get the funding you need when you need it. Putting on our VC hats, here are our best tips.

Two Birds, One VC

What are you raising money for? Team, marketing, distribution? Can you find investors who can help provide you what you need besides capital? At M13, we're not just investing but systematically helping startups scale in less time and with less capital by leveraging our extensive consumer packaged goods (CPG) knowledge and our relationships with partners to help them collectively overcome common industry pain points. There's a lot of capital available today. A lot. Capital is not hard to come by. Your focus should be on finding investors who can actually add value. Here are a few ways we've seen VCs add value:

- Talent/recruiting.
- Introductions, especially to retailers, distributors, advisers, influencers, celebrities, and other investors.
- Strategy. Be careful here. Lots of investors say they're going to help you with strategy. Very few actually have time to do so, so you need to know: (1) Does the investor actually have experience in your space? (2) How much time can he or she really spend with you, and how generous will he or she be with advice? (3) How big an investment are you asking? Will he or she have the bandwidth to help when you need it?

Think Ahead and Work Backward

One piece of advice we repeatedly find ourselves harping on is to work backward from the story you want to be able to tell. What metrics would you need to show investors to get them very excited about your business prospects? Some investors may care more about the absolute number of users on your platform, while others may care more about the percentage of your customers being able to find you organically. Whatever the key metrics are, we recommend using the story you want to tell to guide where you and your team will spend your energy. Ideally, think about which investors you'd like to have in your next round, and find out what they really look for in a business. Then, assuming those metrics align with your vision, focus your team on hitting those milestones before going back to the investors.

Stay in Touch

When you meet a prospective funder, even if you're a year out, send them one or two updates connected to something they care about, so you stay on their radar. Mention who's already invested and how much (or little) room there is left in your round. Investors have FOMO (fear of missing out), too!

Have Your Story Ready

As Carter likes to says, "ABC: Always Be Closing." You never know when you're going to want to circle back, so you better tell a hell of a good story whenever you see them. Rank your possible investors into A, B, and C tiers. Hone your pitch, then start with some C folks so you have time to perfect your pitch, based on their responses. But don't keep all your top picks to the end; there's nothing VCs like less than to feel they're being pitched an overshopped deal. Once you feel you've gotten your pitch down, try some of your A folks.

Consider Corporate Investors

Whom do you think of as your competitors that may instead be great investors? This works better when you have traction, but corporate venture capital (CVC) is growing by leaps and bounds. The five most active CVC companies these days are Google Ventures, Intel Capital, Qualcomm Ventures, Salesforce Ventures, and Comcast Ventures, but there are lots in the consumer space as well. PepsiCo, General Mills, and Kellogg's all now have venture arms, and they're only the tip of the iceberg. Which corporations could make your business if they invested in you? Find them, and use the other tips above. Remember: corporations move slowly, so plan for a long fund-raising process.

EQUITY AND VALUATION BASICS

(If you already know this, feel free to skip ahead.)

If you're taking funding, even from angel friends and family, you need to understand valuation and equity. Valuation can be extremely complicated, but let us break down the basics for you. Valuation is the monetary value of your company and determines the equity stake you give up in exchange for funding. Before each round of funding, a valuation of what the company is worth is calculated. Valuations are arrived at by looking at the management team, track record, market size, and risk. Then percentages of that valuation are given to investors in exchange for funding.

By definition, startups don't have a lot of—or any—financial performance to go on. So valuation is often guesswork on the part of investors. You can influence that number through:

- **Comparables.** Sites such as BizQuest and BizBuySell can provide data on how much similar companies in your industry are worth.
- **Projections.** You can project annual sales and costs, even project how many years to profitability. A company that could be worth $5 million at profitability will be worth some fraction of that number at the startup stage. Be careful about overvaluing your startup with faulty assumptions. It's better to do better than your projections. What are all the assumptions in your model? The key to building projections is to differentiate between facts and assumptions, then set up your assumptions in such a way to project the variety of possible outcomes. We love playing with projections, understanding the assumptions and how realistic they seem, and asking what the business would look like if they were 200 percent off in the positive or negative direction.

The difference between premoney (before funding) valuation and postmoney (after funding) valuation is very important. Let's say an investor agrees to a premoney valuation of $2 million for your company. If he decides to invest $1 million, that makes your company's postmoney valuation $3 million. In this example, the investor's $1 million stake means he now has 33 percent ownership of the company ($1 million divided by $3 million).

Compare that to a situation where your company is valued at $2 million postmoney, indicating a $1 million premoney valuation. This means the investor's $1 million counts as half the company's valuation. She goes away with 50 percent of the company in this scenario, rather than 33 percent. That's a big difference!

THE FOUNDER'S DILUTION DILEMMA

In the beginning, as the founder, you own all the equity in your company. Over time, in addition to giving equity to funders, you may give employees equity in exchange for working for less than the going rate as an incentive to stay. Or to pay for services to attorneys, advisers, and so on, to keep your cash burn rate low. That's just how startups work, whether speedboats or sailboats.

We run into founders all the time who don't want to give up any equity. They shortchange themselves in terms of funding and expertise because they don't want their equity diluted. We call this the founder's dilemma: keeping a small pie all to yourself versus getting a small piece of a much bigger pie.

Of course, everyone's situation is different, but especially if you really want to grow, keeping all the equity is a very shortsighted way to treat your business. Unless you're happy staying supersmall and growing only organically, your goal should be to have the value of your startup increase by enough that your smaller piece is actually worth more.

For example, let's say you own 20 percent of a $2 million company. That means your stake is worth $400,000. If the business does well and you raise an additional $2.5 million of venture capital in a new round at a $7.5 million premoney valuation, which is $10 million postmoney, your stake is diluted by 25 percent ($2.5 million divided by $10 million). Yes, you own less of the company now, but your stake is worth $1.5 million. By taking a lesser percentage, you've created a $1.1 million profit on your investment.

This, of course, is an example of a onetime dilution, and in the startup landscape, companies often raise multiple rounds, which means multiple dilutions. Understanding how you're likely to be diluted over time as your company grows is both important and increasingly complicated. That is why it is important to identify whether you are a speedboat or a sailboat. Though both company types experience dilution, they raise money in different ways and over different time frames. This is why we recommend that you seek professional advice from the start, because each round that your company raises has implications on further funding rounds. You must ensure that there are enough slices of pie to go around.

Four Equity Rules to Live By

1. Treat equity like gold—be cautious about giving it away, because it is literally ownership of your company. On the other hand, if you don't give any away, you're probably not going to grow fast enough. It's a delicate balance.
2. The pie of ownership is fixed, but the value of the company is variable. Owning 100 percent of something worth zero is still worth zero, while owning even .5 percent of an amazing startup could be worth many millions.
3. Know who's motivated by equity and who isn't. You'd think that everyone would want a piece of the upside, but this simply isn't true; everyone has different circumstances and risk tolerance. Don't overlook great talent because he or she isn't motivated by the same potential gain as you are. Some employees, for example, would rather have a larger salary than equity because they need the cash every month.

4. Make equity decisions before the company is worth a lot, and think about the decision as if it already is worth a lot. People tend to wait too long to divide up the pie. Then a difference of 2 percent means a few hundred grand, and suddenly the conversation is a lot harder. On the flip side, don't just throw percentages around in the early days because you think they're not worth anything. Have the conversation early, and take it seriously! This was a potentially sticky issue between the two of us, as Courtney started VEEV before Carter came in, and we worked together for six months before tackling the equity issue. In hindsight we should have figured it out as part of Carter's entry. We had the benefit of being close brothers who weren't going to let it get in the way, but such situations can get ugly.

Obsessively Take Advantage of Your Unfair Advantages: Market Differentiation

A fter graduating from Columbia University, Courtney considered becoming an entrepreneur and turned to our father, the CEO of a large industrial company, for advice. Dad gave it to him straight, the way he always did: "You have no real contacts, no real skill set, and no money. People have done it, but that's what you're up against." As Dad was pointing out, there was no reason why Courtney was better suited to start something than someone else was. He lacked what we today call "unfair advantages." Unfair advantages are assets that you have that others don't that put you into a unique position within a marketplace. They leave competitors saying "I can't believe they have [fill in the blank]! How can we possibly compete with *that*?" As we'll show you in the pages that follow, unfair advantages are essential for startup success today. They create market differentiation, giving you a leg up on competitors.

In less connected and competitive times, being willing to put in hard hours for long enough was usually a recipe for success. Today, everything we're seeing suggests that this is no longer the case. Today's business climate is increasingly specialized and competitive, and moving at lightning speed. You don't have the time to learn everything you need to know in order to succeed, because someone who already knows what you don't can move faster than you. Someone who has the contacts to raise money can do it faster than you can. Someone who has an "in" with the right people in your industry can get their distribution into place sooner than you.

A great example of the power of unfair advantages we talk about all the time is Bouqs, the flower company we seeded four years ago that's a leader in the space. Bouqs applied the direct-to-consumer model to flower delivery, providing fresher flowers for less. Many people had the idea for online floral services. One of the reasons we invested in Bouqs was because one of the founder's families owned a substantial flower farm in Latin America and so had easy access to flowers. In an industry where supply chain access is massively important, Bouqs was able to launch with that core challenge already figured out.

If you were an early competitor of Bouqs and learned of its supply chain ties, wouldn't they feel "unfair" to you? That's exactly what we liked about it as investors. John Tabis and Juan Pablo Montufar didn't have to start from scratch; they were able to leverage experience, family connections, and existing supply chain, vaulting ahead of the competition.

Of course, unfair advantages don't guarantee success. It's easy to say, "Of course Bouqs won the flower space; look at the advantage it had going in." But a lot of people have advantages of one kind or another; very few are able to successfully and aggressively leverage them in creative new ways. That's what today's successful entrepreneurs do. Tabis and Montufar still started small and had to make a lot of correct decisions, surround themselves with the right people, and get quality products to customers. Yes, they had a leg up, but they got a lot else right, too.

To succeed, it's not enough to home in on your unfair advantage; you must then relentlessly exploit it. This is often where people miss their mark. It's like playing blackjack. As experienced players will tell you, the key to winning is getting as much money on the table as possible when you have an advantage against the house and limiting your risk when you don't. Luck also plays a role. But when the dealer's showing a 5 and you have 11, there's no question what you need to do: double down. Relentlessly take advantage of what you have in front of you, because this is your moment.

Unfair advantages generally fall into the categories our dad named: access to the right people relevant to your industry, some specialized skill or knowledge, and/or access to capital. But there are other types as well. In this Switchup, we take you through a process of thinking about what yours are—or could be. Then, in the next chapter, we help you think about maximizing those unfair advantages to up your chances and level of success. First, we'll do a little kimono opening so you can see where we went wrong in the early days of VEEV and how we then went about developing some unfair advantages of our own.

THE BIRTH OF VEEV

Today we won't invest in a business that doesn't have a clear unfair advantage. We're so obsessed with finding unfair advantages because they are exactly what we lacked in our first company.

The liquor business is a notoriously hard one to break into. There's a reason so many liquor companies are started by people whose families are in the liquor industry: the space is uniquely complicated from a distribution and legislative standpoint, and learning to navigate it from scratch is challenging and, in some ways, a fool's errand. We knew no distilleries or distributors, had no experience or connections.

By contrast, early on we met the Cooper brothers, Rob and John. Their father, Robert, had spent most of his life in the adult beverage business, most notably elevating Chambord and selling it to Brown-Forman for a reported $225 million. His son Rob then started St-Germain, an elderflower liqueur, while John started Domaine de Canton, a ginger liqueur. They are both talented in their own right—and helped us learn the ropes along the way—but having the experience and relationships within their family was certainly an unfair advantage. The only advantage we had was Courtney's experience working on the Vitaminwater deal at Goldman Sachs. But the nonalcoholic beverage market is *very* different from the adult beverage market, so it wasn't that much help.

Nonetheless, we dived in headfirst. Courtney assembled a five-page business plan to create and market an açaí-infused liquor called VEEV.

He sent it to people who said they would back him if he ever had a good idea. Within two weeks, he raised a few million dollars from angel investors—our incredible dad, as well as friends and folks we had been lucky to meet through our days at Goldman Sachs. He was off and running, and Carter joined soon after. Carter had just done his time at Goldman and had a brief stint in venture capital in Australia. He had equally limited knowledge of what he was getting into.

Our proposition was simple: people are always going to drink, so let's give them a "better" option—better taste, better ingredients, and better type of company (aka eco-friendly/sustainable). The major categories of alcohol—vodka, gin, whiskey—had been around for centuries, with very little innovation. Our promise to investors was that we could do something innovative within the spirits sector, and the historical exits and multiples paid had rewarded doing so in a very handsome way.

Because we had no unfair advantages, we had to do everything from scratch. From cold-calling distilleries to finding people who could help us turn our homemade blend into a proprietary shelf-stable product and even creating our initial branding materials, we were starting from zero. That is exactly what we want you to avoid. Today's environment is far less forgiving than it was when we began more than ten years ago. Spending a month on something that can take an hour is exactly what you cannot afford to do in today's startup climate.

YOU NEED TO COMPRESS TIME

Unfair advantages help you in many ways, but, most important, they compress time. Here's why that matters so much: imagine that you decide to get into the online flower business the same time Bouqs does; you have the same amount of funding but none of its connections. You have to figure out where you're going to get the flowers. It might take you months to research suppliers, identify them, connect with them, and negotiate a deal to set up your supply chain before you launch your site.

Obviously, starting a business where you already have a supply chain saves you time. What's unique now is how important saving time is when launching a new venture. Given the rate of change and how fast you can generate sales, especially online, once your supply chain is in place, every month you're not live is costlier today than it was five or ten years ago.

The reason is that more customers are discovering new products faster today than they were before. A few years ago, it would take months or years for products to get in front of large swaths of consumers because distribution via brick-and-mortar retail outlets simply took time. Today, it's not just that you can sell online but that there's an increasing number of people who look to discover new things and buy online, perhaps switching from one product to another.

Imagine if you are selling a $10 product and you expect to sell 100 units a day. Not only is every month that goes by when you're not selling costing you $30,000, but you're also providing a window for competitors to acquire the same customers who could be purchasing your goods.

Increased switching rates are one reason that it's important to compress time through unfair advantages. In the United States, companies are struggling to retain customers, as the birthrate of new and better companies has increased. We now exist in a "switching economy" in which the amount of potential revenue that "switches" or transfers from company to company has skyrocketed. One example: a 2015 survey by Accenture of more than 20,000 consumers found that the potential revenue due to increased consumer switching rates has hit the $1.6 trillion mark, a 29 percent increase since 2010.

What's scarier is that customers aren't switching slowly. Look at the chart on the next page, showing BlackBerry's share of the smartphone market. In a period of only five years, BlackBerry went from having over 50 percent of the US market to less than 3 percent. Although Carter still carries around his BlackBerry and is a big fan of the company, his phone serves as a constant reminder that customers can switch on the drop of a dime as consumer options are only increasing, and BlackBerry will not be the last company to see such a rapid decline.

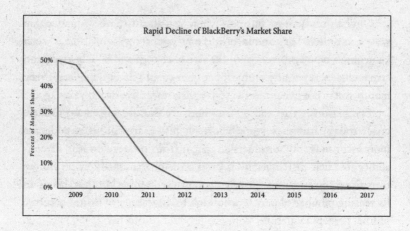

Ease of switching is one reason why today's successful companies all have some kind of unfair advantage, a leg up on the competition that changes the slope of the playing field. If you don't have one, someone else is probably better suited to do what you want to do, because they can move faster and therefore have a higher likelihood of success.

UNFAIR ADVANTAGES CREATE MOMENTUM

When people, whether VCs or customers, see something gaining speed, they want in. Unfair advantages allow you to create momentum earlier than your competitors. Take Jessica Alba, a cofounder of the Honest Company, which is currently worth over $1.5 billion.

In addition to being smart and talented, Jessica had a host of unique advantages to bring to the Honest Company. One was being able to reach tens of millions of individuals just through her own social channels. When she began, she had more than 25 million social media followers. Take a second to think about just how large an advantage this really is. Neutrogena, a major competitor and at the time a more established company, had an Instagram following of only 180,000, which meant that Jessica could reach 138 times the number of people Neutrogena could while spending zero dollars. Such an advantage becomes even more pronounced when you compare her to another startup that would most likely have no followers on day 1.

Jessica's reputation allowed the Honest Company to focus more on selling products and less on building trust in those products because she had credibility with her fan base. For consumer businesses, one of the largest challenges is spreading the word and driving awareness. You can create greater impact if you do it through trusted channels; people are more inclined to buy something if a person they trust endorses it. Jessica's ability to reach millions of people in less time than most people on the planet presented quite a unique advantage. However, her ability to do so while leveraging the trust she'd developed with her fans elevated the Honest Company's efforts significantly. That created momentum, which only increased when Jessica's combination of reach and trust attracted Brian Lee, a seasoned and successful entrepreneur, to the company. Brian had proven prowess and a track record, having founded LegalZoom and ShoeDazzle; his joining then attracted other VCs and talented individuals to the company. The combination of Jessica's and Brian's unfair advantages created a snowball effect, increasing momentum and success.

The OODA Loop

Because acting fast in the startup world means life or death, many companies follow the "OODA loop," a process developed by the military strategist and US Air Force Colonel John Boyd. It has four stages: observe, orient, decide, and act; in other words, collect information, analyze it, determine your course of action, and then execute it. This optimization strategy can help you make speedier, more accurate business decisions. By using a structured approach, you break down complex challenges into manageable actions and make sure you don't miss a step.

You don't need to be a celebrity or an already successful business-person to have unfair advantages. You just need to think about what they could be and how to use them to create momentum. Momentum is built, of course, through sales and increasing the number of key accounts. But it's also created by attracting the right talent, increasing credibility, getting great press, and spreading awareness through your target market.

Social media are a great way to leverage inexpensive tools to showcase the momentum you're building. When people see that acceleration, they become increasingly interested in what you are doing and want to hop on board. But this should not be a "fake it till you make it" situation. If you try to show momentum before you really have any, you're going to invite competitors before your business is defensible. The point is to harness the power of competitive advantages in a strategic way.

WHAT'S YOUR WAR?

If you know the book or movie *Moneyball*, you may remember the concept of WAR, or wins above replacement. The metric was used in scouting and managing to understand a player's contribution to a team relative to an imaginary replacement. Our friend David Lee of Refactor Capital uses this same concept in venture. The point of the method is to consider not just whether someone is valuable but if he or she is more valuable in a given position on a given team relative to other options.

What this means in the context of this Switchup is that you need to assess whether you are the right founder—above other replacement options—to be starting or running this business. Consider the Honest Company again. There are plenty of celebrities who have a larger following than Jessica Alba. For example, Justin Bieber has more than 78 million Facebook followers, which is many more followers than Jessica Alba has. But can you imagine if Justin Bieber were the face of a baby products company? It likely would not have gone as well. The real question is: Were there other celebrities who had a reach equal to or greater than Jessica Alba as well as the same resonance around the products the Honest Company was selling at its start? The answer is "Probably not." Therefore, her WAR score was extremely high.

When we're looking at businesses, we always have this at the top of our minds, both for the "market founder" fit and for us as investors. Is *this* founder the best person to be starting *this* business? Can we add more value to this investment than any other investor can? If not, perhaps we're not best suited to do this deal.

Know what your WAR is as a founder and what kind of WAR you're looking for in investors, team members, celebrity investors, and even vendors. And remember that your first unfair advantage is the hardest to find and leverage. From there, one begets another, and they become easier and easier to create.

BUILD YOUR BUSINESS AROUND YOUR UNFAIR ADVANTAGE

To maximize your WAR, we advocate thinking about your business in a new way. It used to be that you decided to start a company around a product or service, creating a unique selling proposition (USP), also known as a unique value proposition (UVP). VEEV's USP was that it was the world's first alcoholic beverage infused with Brazilian rain forest–grown açaí berries, known to be powerful antioxidants. Furthermore, the drink was packaged in a unique bottle that stood out on liquor store shelves, and each bottle purchased resulted in a donation of $1 to support rain forest protection. That combination was unique, and we got lots of press due to our USP.

Despite our unique USP, turning VEEV into a successful company was an uphill battle because we didn't have strong unfair advantages. That's why we now support flipping conventional thinking on its head: rather than coming up with an idea and then figuring out how to make consumers find it valuable, figure out what you have to offer that consumers will find valuable and use that to create a business.

That's what we've done with M13. Instead of coming up with an idea and then trying to support it with unfair advantages, we started a company *based on* our unfair advantages.

When we started with VEEV, we realized that a major driver of success in the liquor industry is networking and sharing the product with as many influential people as possible. Therefore, we developed a large network of friends and influencers that we could rely on to show up for events, tweet for us, and generally help create the buzz we needed to be featured in media.

We didn't set out to create VEEV in order to develop a strong network of influencers; it was an unintended consequence, but one that we can now leverage beyond VEEV. In addition to developing a strong network of contacts, we gained operating and investing experience, as well as access to information in the worlds of branding, investing, and consumer products. We're now playing with the ways to connect all of those dots in a repeatable and scalable fashion as M13 invests in and develops businesses at the nexus of consumer products and consumer technology. We are essentially leveraging the unfair advantages we built during and since VEEV to ensure that M13 offers something different and attractive to young brands and businesses.

You probably also have some unfair advantages from whatever work you've done in the past. The point here is that you increase your WAR when you form your business and your USP around them.

DETERMINING YOUR UNFAIR ADVANTAGES

You may not have been born with obvious unfair advantages, but that doesn't mean you don't have them. Here are some things to consider when looking for them.

- What do your friends, colleagues, and acquaintances come to you for? Whether or not you are officially an expert in something, what do people see you as a thought leader in?
- If you had to make $1,000 in the fastest possible (legal) way, what would you do?
- Who are the five most successful people you know? What are they successful in, and if you were they, how would you leverage their skill or foundation further? Have you brought this idea to them?

- If you had to focus on one activity for the next ten years, what would it be?

  Additional questions if you're already up and running:

- Where is your highest concentration of revenue?
- Where do you spend the least amount of your time with the best results? That is, what's the lowest-hanging fruit?
- If you had an extra two hours each day to grow your business, not catch up, where would you spend it?
- Who are your most profitable customers? What part of your offering would be hardest for them to find elsewhere?

OTHER PLACES TO LOOK FOR YOUR UNFAIR ADVANTAGE

So far in this chapter, we've alluded to three big types of advantages: access to capital, specialized knowledge, and connections with powerful people who can help you. But there are all kinds of advantages that can differentiate you as a founder. Here are some to consider.

Vantage Point

Is there something about your position in your job, your church, or your friend group that gives you a unique vantage point to catch trends? That was the case with the Chia Company. It started as a family farm in Australia, which at the time was the only place in the world where chia was being grown. Founder John Foss was a farmer and scientist by trade. He saw the demand for chia increasing at exponential rates and reached out to other farmers to combine forces and corner the market on chia. They used their vantage point as suppliers to see the growing demand to get the jump on other regions such as Mexico and South America, which soon caught on to the chia craze. Are you in a position to spot trends early? If so, what might you be able to do to get ahead of those trends?

Here's another example: the makers of KeVita created a refreshing, low-calorie drink that delivered probiotics in a liquid product years before anyone else. Previously, probiotics were available only in pill form at health food stores or in foods such as yogurt. KeVita cofounder Bill Moses was a winemaker who was familiar with the process of fermentation required to produce probiotics. He lived in the Ojai region of Southern California, where many food and beverage trends start, and he began hearing more and more about probiotics. Since he understood the production processes, he was able to marry his background with the trends he spotted. As a side note, he was very smart to start as a sailboat and not try to be a speedboat, because consumers were just beginning to catch on to probiotics.

Our take: You may have more advantages than you currently think. What Bill Moses shows us is that you have to pay attention in order to see them and know how to use them. In some ways, this is no different from Malcolm Gladwell's "outliers" and his famous dissection of Bill Gates's good fortune. Gates grew up in Seattle during the time that he did with the parents he had. Although the other Bill (Moses) is not Bill Gates, he's now an incredibly successful entrepreneur because he took advantage of his surroundings to create his own luck. "Chance favors the prepared," as they say. Bill was prepared.

Manufacturing Process

Having a proprietary manufacturing process or access to an existing supply chain like Bouqs' can provide a uniquely competitive advantage. We've seen this take many forms. In some cases, founders take an existing manufacturing plant or excess plant capacity and apply it to a new product. For example, our friend Pat Turpin, the founder of Popchips, a healthful potato chip company, worked for Costco before finding a rice cake plant that he would eventually go on to purchase. He used the factory to develop a new product with higher demand. Popchips was still a startup—but one with economies of scale in manufacturing that typical startups lack.

Where are you thinking of manufacturing your product? Is there a way you can take a different approach so you start with an advantage?

Brand

It's not surprising that Tyra Banks started an entertainment, beauty, and fashion company, right? She's spent her whole life modeling and then producing and starring in a TV show on modeling. Celebrities usually do this kind of thing well; they leverage their fame to create companies or help build products related to what they're known for. Even if you're not a celebrity, you can ask yourself, "What do people know me for?" even if it's just people from your neighborhood.

Here's an example. Keith Ferrazzi, the author of *Never Eat Alone and Other Secrets to Success, One Relationship at a Time*, rose through the ranks of the consulting firm Deloitte. When he was deciding what company to start, he thought about what he was best known for and where he had the most connections. The answer was with leaders in talent and human resources, especially at Fortune 500 companies. So he set out to solve one of their biggest pain points: hiring and keeping great employees. His new company, Yoi Corporation, provides SaaS-based (software as a service) mobile digital tools for managers that help with onboarding and employee engagement, evaluation and performance management, training and development, and exiting. He took what he did as a consultant and turned it into software that he could sell to his old clients. That way he could leverage the brand he'd created for years across his entire network.

The point here is that when you're looking for your own company to start, think creatively, but also think as close to home as possible. Think about what you know and what people know you for. There's a lot to figure out when you're starting something new. Don't make starting a company harder than it already is by increasing the number of unknowns. Don't worry, you'll still have plenty of adventure and risk!

Influencers

Influencers are people who have large networks and can spread the word about your product or service. It's easy to think, "I don't know any celebrities," but influencers are different for every business and every customer. They don't have to be famous, but they must be sources of information relevant to your product or service whom your customers trust.

Take Thrive Market: some of its biggest influencers are regular folks with big followings on Pinterest, Twitter, or their own blogs who simply love to post about food and drinks. An insight here is that we look to different people for different things. People might look to Floyd Mayweather for recommendations on entertainment and where to find a good boxing gym but not on where to find the right accountant. People might trust Jessica Alba's endorsement of diapers but not men's razors.

Who are your customers, and what are you selling to them? You may not know any celebrities, but who in your network influences a group of people about what you are selling?

One company that has taken this approach to become successful is Mayvenn, an e-commerce site that sells hair extensions targeting the African American market. Its directors realized that their unfair advantage was that they had access to a network of the best stylists for African Americans, who could influence which products customers bought. So they created a revenue model in which stylists refer clients to the Mayvenn site and get a commission on every purchase, earning as much as an extra $2,000 per month. Do you think stylists enthusiastically refer clients to Mayvenn's products? You *bet*.

UNFAIR ADVANTAGES

So far, we've suggested places to look to find your advantages. If you still can't see any, it's time to create them. One of the most obvious is by partnering with someone who has them. We're seeing this play out in consumer products more and more. Founders are bringing in retailers as investors, as opposed to just distribution partners.

In the old days, once you developed your product, you'd spend large amounts of time, money, and energy to get the biggest retailers to carry it. Today, savvy founders are offering a portion of the business to retailers in exchange for shelf space and in-store promotion. Imagine if, instead of asking Target to carry your product in its stores, you offered

Target 10 percent of your company if it would put it in all their stores. Unfair advantage paradigm shift!

Where else could you apply this? Can you lock up supply by finding the largest supplier and getting it to invest in your business? It may sound counterintuitive, but think collaboratively. For instance, when Lauren Bush was launching FEED, she did so with a few big and well-known brands, such as GAP and Barnes & Noble, helping her get the word out from the get-go and giving these brands an opportunity to associate with a great cause.

Another example of a relatively easy place to create unfair advantages is in crowdfunding, an increasingly popular way to finance your company, business extension, or project. Crowdfunding does not just need to be a prelaunch strategy. One of our portfolio companies, Hylete, uses crowdfunding to prefund production. When it conceptualizes a new product, it launches a crowdfunding campaign to test the waters and see how consumers respond. If a product doesn't have high uptake, it simply doesn't manufacture it. The company has now built a loyal social following that basically acts as a testing ground for its products.

Whatever you are using crowdfunding for, how can you launch a campaign and stand out from the crowd? Here are some ideas for creating unfair advantages.

- Use the right platform. CircleUp, Kickstarter, StartEngine, Crowd-funder, and Indiegogo—all have their own specialties. Be sure to do your research about which crowdsourcing platforms are strongest in the category you hope to enter. Each has a different resonance with different audiences.
- Get the platform behind you. Similar to bringing in Target as an investor, can you get your chosen platform or a platform expert behind you for equity or revenue sharing? As a rule of thumb, we try to avoid consultants or business partners who are unwilling to take risk alongside us. By offering upside, you encourage your partners to have a vested interest in your long-term success—and not in that of your competition. A bouillon cube company that we like,

called BOU, has taken on this strategy. BOU offers low-sodium flavor cubes that help enhance the flavor profiles of all sorts of dishes, from soups to risottos. When the founder of BOU discovered that one particular manufacturer specializes in the technology necessary to produce its cubes, rather than entering a typical manufacturer-to-business relationship, he thought of a different way to set up the deal, eventually leading to the manufacturer's direct investment in BOU. The company's savvy founder found a way to get a platform behind him and stack the deck in his favor.

- Build momentum ahead of time. Court your friends, family, and anyone else you can think of to donate as soon as your campaign goes live. That way, by the time you start promoting the campaign, you're already demonstrating momentum. Momentum really matters in crowdfunding; people want to jump in if they feel you're taking off. As a rule of thumb, don't launch a crowdfunded campaign with less than 25 percent of your campaign prefunded.

- Cross-promote with winners. Reach out to leading campaigns and offer to cross-promote. With less momentum, you may need to offer more, such as posting twice for each one of their posts, but it is crucial to build your following in the early days.

Creating unfair advantages is all about stacking the deck in your own favor—finding ways to proactively reduce risk and increase upside. That's what good entrepreneurs do. Have you thought of an unfair advantage you can leverage? Do you see how you can begin to create one or more? Maybe you've even thought of a new business idea based on something special you have. It's time to turn to Switchup 4 and see how to use your unfair advantage to its fullest potential.

PART 2
RUNNING THE BUSINESS

Do What You Do Best, and Outsource the Rest: Specialization

This Switchup is about the importance of homing in on what you do best and giving up control in the areas where others are better. It highlights one of our fundamental principles: that the best outcomes occur when everyone does what he or she does best. As we've mentioned previously, speed is one of the most important keys to success today. One of the best ways to move fast is to outsource the functions that are not within your sweet spot.

This sounds simple, but we don't commonly see it practiced. Many founders continue to insist on building their vision from the ground up, handling all the "important functions" to make sure they get it right. That's certainly the traditional way entrepreneurs have grown businesses: come up with a great idea, gather money, find a space, develop the product or service, figure out how to make, distribute, and sell it, build a team, create a website, and develop a social media presence. In this typical startup mentality, you build out all the aspects of a business— responding to needs like a game of whack-a-mole. It's time-consuming and, in an increasingly complex and specialized world, unrealistic.

As first-time entrepreneurs with VEEV, we followed that traditional route, building every part of the business from the ground up. In hindsight, we realized we had been doing it all wrong. Why reinvent the wheel when there are folks out there who know how to make parts of the wheel better than we ever could? We experienced how much time, money, and energy it takes to build from scratch—and that was at a time with more forgiving timelines. We learned the hard way that nothing takes more energy than trying to do well that which you are naturally bad at. That's how we came up with this Switchup: focus on what you do best, and partner, collaborate, license, and outsource *everything else.* Though that may seem counterintuitive, at one of the most competitive times ever in history, we believe the answer lies in collaboration.

We're so committed to this Switchup that we created our new company, M13, based on it. Our business model is predicated on teaming up with talented executors and best-in-class partners, rather than on employees and contractors. With VEEV we hired a person every time we had—or thought we had—a need. With M13, we plan to outsource and partner as much as possible while maintaining a small, dynamic team that can, above all else, manage processes instead of projects. With fewer than twenty-five employees, we believe we can repeatedly launch and scale businesses by working with top-tier partners at every step of the value chain, rather than trying to do everything ourselves. By allowing each party to focus entirely on what it does best, we're able to accelerate growth faster and with less risk than most brands could on their own.

A Cautionary Note

There's a tension here regarding outsourcing and partnering that we've had a lot of conversations about: What and when to outsource? What and when to partner? As we said in Switchup 1, we believe in doing as much as possible yourself at the very beginning, because there are key things that you have to experience yourself. But as soon as you have mined your experience for insights and strategies, you should outsource the nonessentials.

We're not alone in focusing on our strengths and outsourcing everything else. Using this principle, many businesses are now quickly scaling to $100 million and above. Here's a recent example of a startup that really took off when it adopted this concept. Surf Air is a startup that originally began by offering unlimited flights for a fixed monthly fee. It was well capitalized, and owned and operated all of its planes. Within a few years, however, the directors realized that operating a fleet was not their core competency—management and marketing was. Retrenching around their main strength, they sold 100 percent of their planes to a third-party operator and then leveraged the operator as a partner.

Surf Air's ability to take advantage of this Switchup has allowed the company to grow and scale rapidly. In fact, Surf Air's recent expansion into Europe, offering unlimited air travel between major European cities to businesses and consumers, would not have been possible if it had had to purchase an entire new fleet. Turning the airline into an asset-light, global membership business, with local aircraft operating partners in each market, has provided Surf Air with a completely different scalability profile.

Overall, focusing on your unfair advantages and outsourcing the rest increases your likelihood of success and decreases the chances of failure. A counter case in point is the Chia Company. As we mentioned in Switchup 3, John Foss set up a world-class global chia supply chain, creating economies of scale and a major unfair advantage. Unfortunately, the Chia Company ran into trouble when its directors decided to venture too far up the value chain and become a consumer brand. It spent time and dollars on marketing rather than being an industrial supplier for consumer brands, leveraging its unfair advantage, and letting other companies fill in the gaps.

The Chia Company is just one example, but today it's harder than ever to own multiple parts of the supply chain. Vertical integration is especially tough when the cost of starting businesses is so low and new players are constantly entering the market.

The flip side of this problem is part of what makes this Switchup possible—the amount of infrastructure that already exists across most supply chains in the United States. This is still not true for all other parts of the world. If you wanted to start a snack company in many developing countries, for instance, it's likely that you would have to build the entire supply chain yourself. That is both time-consuming and capital intensive.

In the United States and other industrialized countries, however, no matter what you're doing, there are usually plenty of strong partners throughout the value chain. We believe that the game these days is all about creating the minimum amount of new infrastructure necessary to take advantage of your unfair advantages—unless your advantage is infrastructure, in which case we would suggest you leverage that! Otherwise, you are creating unnecessary and expensive redundancies. For instance, Thrive Market and Amazon are increasingly go-to launch partners for distribution, which alleviates the need for companies to build up their own e-commerce website. Or let's say that your company is in need of cloud storage: you can shop offers from Microsoft, Amazon, Verizon, Rackspace, and many more. As Courtney says, "The future is here, but it is not evenly distributed."

ADVANTAGES OF OUTSOURCING

As the example of Surf Air shows, this Switchup offers all kinds of strategic advantages. It allows for speed: you don't waste time creating systems that already exist somewhere else. It keeps you lean, which means you need less investment to get a minimum viable product (MVP) out the door. It significantly reduces your capital requirements, one of the most common inhibitors to startup growth. It allows you to get to market and then scale quickly, because you are teaming up with viable businesses that are already at scale. As a result, this Switchup changes the risk profile of starting a company.

Another key advantage to this partnering approach is that it creates competitive excellence, because you can focus on doing what you are great at. There is an increased need for specialization when you're trying to move fast and be best in class. People do their best work when they're working on what they are great at. When you find ways to structure projects around each party's unfair advantages, the combined result is a faster process and a higher-quality product.

We think of it like a Hollywood film production model. To make a blockbuster, you need a best-in-class director, a major producer, a cinematographer, writers, actors, set designers, costume designers, and so on. Imagine if you tried to make a film where you had the same person running all the major parts of production. If that person did a good job, it'd be impressive, but if he or she did a good job and was able to do it fast, that'd be a shock. Be the producer of your business, and find the talent and partners you want to help you make your movie.

When you haven't done something before, you're going to take longer to do it for the first time. On the flip side, if you've done something many times before, there are economies of scale on everything from the equipment you use to your knowledge of how to do it well. Not only will you accomplish the task faster, but you will also have a higher probability of success. If you can find best-in-class partners that can save you time and provide higher quality, they tend to make up in speed and quality what they cost in dollars.

SYMBIOTIC PARTNERSHIPS

It's not just startup founders who need to figure out what they do best and what to outsource; big companies do, too. As companies become successful, they tend to do more and more functions in-house to retain control and because they believe it's cheaper at a certain scale. In many cases, they're right. But with size come slowness and a mentality that's typically not one of rigorously testing and iterating. Piloting a big ship is very different from piloting a speedboat. Given the need to be more flexible in this day and age for all the reasons we've named, it's not surprising that corporations are trying to think and act more like startups.

Why is this important? Corporations need you. In fact, a 2016 survey showed that 82 percent of corporations are looking to learn from or partner with startups as a means of increasing innovation (see the chart below). In the past, corporations could crush new entrants trying to enter their spaces. It's harder to do that now, because lower startup costs allow more companies to enter the market and it's hard to fight wars on multiple fronts. So corporations are increasingly trying to partner with, invest in, or buy startups to prevent disruption and ensure innovation. If you can't beat 'em, join 'em, as they say.

That's why it's more advantageous for you as a founder to look at corporations not as the enemy you want to disrupt but as a potential mutually beneficial partner to help you scale faster. It's a completely different mind-set and approach, but one with potentially "unfair" outcomes.

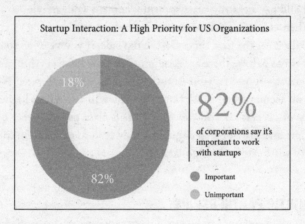

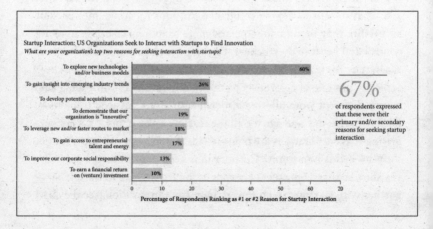

Nordstrom has been on a tear recently, creating partnerships with startups from Bonobos and HauteLook to Warby Parker. Similarly, major retailers such as Target have been making an effort to partner with high-potential startups such as Cash Warren's Pair of Thieves. We are huge fans of Pair of Thieves, which originally launched offering a better sock but has reinvigorated the sock and underwear category, catching the eyes of Millennials and eventually large corporations such as Target. Those companies could have tried to fight Nordstrom. Instead, they're seeing Nordstrom as a valuable channel to help them reach further scale. Remember, e-commerce still accounts for less than 15 percent of total retail sales in the United States, meaning that brick-and-mortar retailers continue to drive huge volume.

Don't minimize the reach of the big guys, but also don't forget that you as an innovator have something very powerful to offer them. *All companies* need to figure out how to take advantage of their unfair advantages and outsource the rest—and that means there are all types of possibilities for partnerships, collaborations, and joint ventures. As we always say, "Figure out how to make yourself indispensable"—that's the key.

This new way of thinking can be difficult for the typical entrepreneur, who is used to going solo. We know a seasoned entrepreneur who'd just launched his most recent tech company when he got a call from a Fortune 50 company. "We've heard about what you're doing and want to do something similar," the corporate CEO said. "We're too busy with other priorities to do it ourselves. Do you want to partner with us?" The entrepreneur's first inclination was to say no. He wanted to beat the big guy, not join 'em. And he certainly wasn't excited about giving up control. Who knew what a partnership with that company would turn out like? Upon reflection, he decided to say yes, and he was immediately approached by some of the best investors in the business, who now wanted in. He has yet to produce anything, but as a result of that partnership, his company was suddenly valued at more than $20 million.

We want you not just to answer "yes" to such requests if they come (they're not very common) but to actively pursue the creation of such deals from the start. Thinking in this way will affect everything about the way you do business: what you keep control of, what you outsource, what kind of team and infrastructure you build. It begins by understanding a simple yet profound economic principle, which we cover next.

OPPORTUNITY COST

Opportunity cost is a crucial factor that many founders fail to fully take into account when they say, "I need to do it all by myself." It's defined as the loss of potential gain from other alternatives when one alternative is chosen. In other words, when you spend your time and money on one thing, by definition you can't spend it on something else, so you're losing the potential value of the other choice. Opportunity costs can be monetary, but they can also include lost time, output, attention, or any other benefit to your company that you could have had if you'd made a different choice. Time and attention are finite, so when you choose to do one thing, you're always forgoing the value you could have created by doing something else.

Let's imagine your unfair advantage is that you do killer product design and you've decided to do it the old way: by building out all the parts of the business yourself. Just think of the number of products you could design with the time and money you will spend on creating an e-commerce site to sell product number one, rather than partnering with an existing site that could carry all the products you design. That's the power of opportunity costs!

You want to think through this concept very carefully, because it can mean the razor's edge difference between success and failure. Your job is to figure out which opportunities are the best ones for you to leverage and which are the ones to outsource. Partly because the concept of opportunity cost is conjecture—how can you tell what you will lose by not taking a certain path?—and partly because founders can be stubborn individualists, this is a common and potentially huge startup mistake.

Recently, Courtney and Peter Maldonado, the founder of Chomps Snack Sticks, a meat sticks company producing 100 percent grass-fed, gluten-free, paleo-friendly meat snacks, were discussing a partnership. A strong entrepreneur, Peter had built Chomps into a $10 million–plus business by himself. When Courtney and Peter spoke, they discussed how incredible the journey to $10 million had been and about the value of a partnership with M13. With retail, supply chain, and media experience, Courtney believed that the M13 team could accelerate Chomps's near-term growth by at least six months. In the crowded meat stick category, this could give Chomps a serious advantage, and that's exactly why Chomps and M13 began working together.

START WITH WHAT YOU DO BEST

There's a huge difference among good, better, and best in every aspect of business, and being best in class gives you a significant competitive advantage. In the last chapter, you looked at your unfair advantages, so you should already have some idea of what piece of the business you're best at and therefore should control or develop. Here we'll give you some other ways to think about it.

Start with yourself. What makes you great? Is it as an inventor, the creator of a brand-new product that no one has ever thought about before? Is it your ability, like the tech guy, to see where technology is going and put together a nimble team of developers to get there faster than other people can? Is it your amazing stickiness on social media? Your ability to tell a story and get people's buy-in? Whatever it is, it's your key differentiator, the thing you must keep control of. For instance, if your unfair advantage is that you are a scientist who comes up with revolutionary product formulas, that's the part of the business you should be focusing on.

Then think about your team. What previous experience do your team members have? What are the strengths and unfair advantages of your team?

Next, think about your company and industry. What is the most important part of the value chain to control? Which parts are commoditized, and which are not? What have competitors outsourced versus owned, and how did they perform?

Even the US Postal Service is beginning to think this way. What's it best at? Though this may be questionable, it would say delivery. More specifically, it has built the infrastructure for nationwide delivery. It has staff, trucks, and systems in place. So it partnered with Amazon to deliver parcels, and now it's responsible for nearly 40 percent of Amazon deliveries. "It's just leveraging our infrastructure," says Megan Brennan, the current postmaster general.

Finding "Your Best"

Make a list right now ranking the five things you do best, then prioritize by your greatest unfair advantages. What pattern do you observe? Are numbers one, two, and three tied together? What can you see cutting across all three? Then focus on those and think about how to outsource the others. But let's say that numbers two and three have nothing to do with number one but numbers four and five do; perhaps you should think about how you can get better at numbers four and five or how you might bundle them with number one and outsource numbers two and three. Don't even think about not outsourcing *something*.

OUTSOURCE THE REST

Once you know what you should focus on, you start to think about how to outsource the rest. If you're a great product designer, you shouldn't be trying to build a manufacturing plant or an e-commerce site to sell your product. There are people who are already doing those things faster, better, and cheaper than you can. Your job is to find them.

Besides manufacturing and e-commerce, think about every single aspect of your business, from the office (no, you don't need your own, and yes, we share our office with another startup) to infrastructure and the creation, manufacturing, selling, and marketing of your idea. Some things are obvious, such as finding a customer acquisition expert. But here are a few categories you might not have considered.

The Business Concept Itself

Behind a lot of this Switchup is horizontal thinking: How can you layer what you're doing on top of something that already exists? Lyft is a great example. In the past, it would have bought its own cars and started a transportation network. Instead, it became a software and marketing platform to facilitate other people being their own transportation fleet. Airbnb is the same. In the old model, Marriott and other chains built and bought hotels and rented hotel rooms. Airbnb saw that there were already "hotel" rooms out there in people's houses and created a platform for folks to leverage that resource. Like those companies, is your idea something that could add on to some existing infrastructure and make it easier or smarter or even create a whole new market?

The Last Mile

"The last mile" is an expression that refers to the last leg of any purchase: warehousing inventory and delivering it to consumers. That is an easy outsource. Why would you carry inventory in a warehouse or do fulfillment when you can have Amazon, Jet.com, or Thrive Market do it for you? Yes, it will cost you, but it will extend your reach to far corners of the country without your having to establish and maintain giant distribution warehouses, freeing you up to do what you do best.

Last-mile options include delivery companies such as Instacart for groceries and UberEATS for restaurant orders. Drones are hovering on the horizon for this, as well. Howard Schultz thinks we'll all have our Starbucks orders delivered to us within the next few years. Carter is a trendsetter: he has his Starbucks orders delivered through an experimental partnership among Starbucks, Postmates, and Lyft.

Talent

Of course, you need to work with the best people who complement your strengths. But do you really need employees? A lot more people have side hustles these days. You can take advantage of that to find experienced folks to work with—according to CareerBuilder, 60 percent of workers over the age of sixty will be looking for a new job after retiring.

In the past, you would think, "I need to hire someone to run supply chain management for me." These days, you can find a supply chain partner who's offering those services or a person who's the greatest at supply chain management and who already has a job. You can hire her to consult with you on a per project basis. She may be interested in doing it for a fee and perhaps a little equity, but also because she wants to be involved with a cool idea.

This approach can save you a lot of money and get you higher-quality talent than you might otherwise be able to attract. CFO, for instance, is a role that is typically filled on a project or part-time basis at most startups. You can get really seasoned pros who are willing to give you their expertise this way. You can find such people at, for example, B2B CFO and CFO for Rent, and there are more on our website, www.shortcutyourstartup.com.

Whom you decide to have in-house depends on what you are focusing on. We never had an in-house designer for VEEV, because we could get access to better talent by outsourcing. If we had been a design company, then of course we would have had the designer in-house. What's your team makeup, and does it accurately reflect the percentage of time you want to spend on each activity your business does?

Teaming with Another Startup

Say you have an idea for female yoga wear, and you meet a person who has an idea for a men's CrossFit brand. From the minute you have your ideas, you're trying to solve the same problems. You have to design the product, source it, figure out the best team to come up with the logo, decide how to sell the product online, acquire customers, build the brand . . . so why not do it together or at least consolidate the back end? Sharing the burden will reduce the cost and time tremendously. Have you ever seen a Baskin-Robbins, Dunkin' Donuts, and Subway sharing the same retail location? They are separate entities, but they've seen the value of consolidating the back end, saving costs while maintaining their separate brands. There are many opportunities to do this today, even in digital businesses.

RESOURCES FOR PARTNERING

Here are some of our favorite resources for finding the right partners and outsourcers. Of course, don't underestimate the power of your own social media network. We know of one entrepreneur who found the perfect partner for her media business with just one phone call to a friend of a friend, which resulted from a Facebook connection.

Partnership Platforms

You can think of a partnership platform as a "matchmaker." There are a variety of such platforms to choose from. For example, DojoMojo is a company that facilitates partnerships to help grow your email subscriber list. Partnered, which has gotten a lot of press lately, is another. There's a boatload more of our favorite partnership platforms at www.shortcutyourstartup.com.

Media and PR

We love LUMAscapes, a company that puts together maps of media partners and PR agencies to help you figure out how to navigate all the options. It's a pipeline for similar best-in-class resources.

Information Technology

Similarly, GitHub is a website where you can find coders, and ZipRecruiter is a great tool for any type of recruiting.

NEGOTIATE DEALS BY ALIGNING INCENTIVES

Once you've found the right folks to partner with, it's time to make a deal. Don't go in blind. Research everything you can about their business, and have a view on what their pain points are. Think long term and think of the ZOPA (Zone of Possible Agreement). We learned this term from Deepak Malhotra, one of our favorite professors at Harvard Business School. The essence is to look for deals that are "win-wins" for both sides and grow the overall pie. These are the types of agreements that lead to long-term value and relationships. The days of one-sided deals are becoming obsolete in the connected, globalized world, because reputations travel fast. So many deals do not get done because people are thinking too short term. Good partnerships rarely pay off in the short term, but they shine long term and create an opportunity for future deals in which both parties find value.

Try to align incentives so that you pay as little as possible up front. Focus on finding the triple win: you win, I win, and the customer wins. It's not that you want everything for free. It's more that you're going to help the other party win because you understand its objectives. It's going to help you win, because it understands yours. When we align them, we all prosper.

You can use this kind of thinking no matter how small your business is. Let's say you need a pop-up retail space. Walk down a cool street, find a building that's not leased, call the owner and say, "I'll give you 2 percent of the sales for the next ninety days if I can try this out here." You're not spending anything up front, and the owner is making some money on an otherwise vacant building.

Or let's say you want an influencer with a large social following to post something about your product or service. Oftentimes, people will pay in cash for that, say $1,000. An alternative we use is to offer a $1,000 gift certificate for Carbon 38, one of the companies we're invested in that's a really popular female clothing line. The people at Carbon 38 give us a discount if they know an influencer is going to buy something and is likely to post it on social media. That's a win for the influencer, for Carbon 38, and for us. What can you offer? Think about it a little bit more creatively, and all of a sudden, you'll be aligning everyone's interests.

Do Deals on the Margin

It's best to structure deals on the margin or as a percentage of net sales, rather than on a fixed price. That way, everyone has skin in the game and is incentivized to work as a team for the best possible outcome. Additionally, you're not locked into a number you might not be able to deliver on. If we had to write a $1 million check because we'd agreed to give someone 40 percent margin, we'd happily do it because that means we grossed $2.5 million.

KEEP YOUR EYE ON THE BALL

Remember that just because you outsource something, it doesn't mean you don't keep an eye on it. You may have given that piece of responsibility away because you're not the best at it, but ideally you're involved and overseeing it. There's a fine line between staying focused on your unfair advantage and letting other folks do whatever they want to. As our dad used to say, "What gets measured, gets managed." This is why at M13 we are so focused on finding and selecting the right partners to work with, managing our relationships with them, and making decisions with as much information as possible. If there is one lesson that we have taken away from our work with VEEV, it is to not make decisions in a vacuum.

STOP CRADLING YOUR PRECIOUS IDEA

Before we bring this chapter to a close, we want to mention one more thing: a crucial implication of this Switchup is that you can't be afraid to share your idea. Too many entrepreneurs get hung up here, worrying about someone stealing their concept.

We now live in an open-source world, one that requires transparency in everything: from where your clothes come from to where the meat in your burger or your coffee beans come from. It used to be that you guarded your secret recipe in a safe and never told others what you were working on, for fear they would copy it.

We believe those days are over. In the startup world, sharing is not just encouraged, it's expected. First, as we've said, it's almost guaranteed that at least one other person is working on your idea. Second, because of the interconnected world, it's almost impossible for people not to know what you're working on relatively early, even if you try to keep it under wraps. Third, you must talk about your idea to get crucial feedback. If you don't get input from others who are knowledgeable about the industry or your potential customers, your idea may remain stale or lack innovation.

These days it's better and, frankly, easier to win out in the open by collaborating with others. Ideas are worth nothing unless they are well executed. Your best defense is to hook up with quality people and companies and move fast, so that other people don't even think of coming after you.

No matter what ecosystem you are in, the best thing you can do is to surround yourself with great people and the materials you need to win. The world's never been more connected, as demonstrated by the fact that the average American has more than three Internet-connected devices. There are just so many more ways for people and brands to share and collaborate than ever before. The more you can bring great companies together, the more media attention you can get, the more eyeballs you can attract, the more social sharing you can generate.

One additional reason for collaborating that we haven't yet mentioned: when you work with other people, especially experts in their fields, you get the benefits of all the conversations you're having that enrich your thinking. The advantage of that kind of exposure can't be overestimated—because remember, the main thing that doesn't scale is a person's time. Don't compete, collaborate.

Build in Flexibility and a Diversified Focus: Iterations and Pivots

When we started, VEEV stood for Vitamin Enhanced Energy Vodka. Yes, after spending time overseas and seeing how people were mixing Red Bull and vodka, our original idea was to put vitamins into vodka and create an enhanced liquor. However, we quickly found that to be a difficult undertaking, as liquor laws prohibited such products. That didn't discourage us, and as we continued to think about it, we began to see that "energy" was just one type of benefit and that there was room for a "better" alcoholic beverage. Using the concept of better, we landed on: better ingredients, better taste, and a better, more sustainable company.

Moving along with our concept of "better," we chose to classify VEEV as a liquor, instead of as a vodka. However, as we noted earlier, classifying VEEV that way proved problematic, as consumers often confused it with a "liqueur." That was a serious problem because we were looking to target a wide audience and liqueurs are typically associated with older drinkers. To alleviate confusion, we started using a new phrase to describe VEEV: "The world's first açaí spirit that mixes and drinks like a vodka." Customers responded positively to that, given their familiarity with mixing vodka drinks.

As we continued to interact with and listen to customers, we received consistent feedback. People would say, "I love VEEV, but I don't feel it. It's just not strong enough." Our consumers were looking for a higher-proof (higher alcohol percentage) beverage—that is, more bang for their buck. We responded by raising the proof and ultimately reformulated VEEV to be closer to vodka, making it more mixable and even more popular with mixologists, who responded even better to the new product.

As you can see from our experience with VEEV, listening to customers and transforming as you go is a crucial requirement for startup success. Though this may seem intuitive, such flexibility was not always valued so highly. The old entrepreneurial approach was to decide on your course of action and focus on that product or service exclusively. You created a plan, then put your head down and stuck to it relentlessly. You knew where you were heading, and your job was to get through any obstacle to get there—running through walls no matter what.

Because the world has become so complex, today an entrepreneur can't afford to have such single-mindedness. Markets, consumer behaviors, and technologies are all evolving over shorter time frames than ever before. If you look down for too long, something from a competitor or an entirely new market may emerge, leaving your product or company in the dust.

These days, success goes not to the entrepreneur who gets it right off the bat but to the one who continually evolves his or her organization to meet the changing needs of consumers. Whereas in the past the ability to "run through walls" may have been a sought-after trait in founders, today dexterity and adaptability are two of the most important traits of successful entrepreneurs.

As Carter often says, "Running through walls doesn't scale." That's because this process is usually inefficient and leaves you or your team with less energy to surmount the next obstacle. Most importantly, charging hard through obstacles makes it difficult to pause and to truly understand the problem. Select cases may require brute force and perseverance to get through—for instance, leaning on your suppliers or manufacturers to deliver product on time. However, in most cases, your challenges are symptoms of poor product/market fit, founder/market fit, or storytelling. When it comes to these types of challenges, trying to run through walls without getting to the core of the problem will only hurt you later.

Instead of charging hard down a planned course, in most cases we recommend pausing frequently and briefly to develop new strategies. Running through walls requires commitment and conviction, but so does having the discipline to pause and think deeply when you hit a roadblock. You still need a huge amount of energy, but instead of expending it on aimless sprints, direct it at thoughtful problem solving, data-driven decision making, and strategic adjustments. When you do this correctly, you will get to the bottom of complex challenges and find solutions that scale. You will lead your company to a better place.

Though flexibility has always been an important part of the process, today it is absolutely critical. In his book *The Third Wave: An Entrepreneur's Vision of the Future*, AOL cofounder and former CEO Steve Case emphasizes the importance of flexibility in explaining his thoughts on entering the third wave of the Internet. He explains that after building the infrastructure in the first wave and then creating the applications on top of it in the second, we are currently entering a new phase, in which we are working to integrate the Internet into every aspect of our lives in seamless and invisible ways. Case's road map to help people navigate through the third wave is grounded in keeping a wide perspective, iterating, and leveraging insights. That's the essence of this Switchup.

This way of working requires seeing every challenge not as a test of your intelligence but as an opportunity to enhance your company, your product or service, and yourself. The story of the evolution of Meerkat epitomizes this approach. The app Meerkat was a side project of an Israeli tech firm called Life on Air. It was the company's third attempt at a live video application. When Meerkat rapidly gained traction, Life on Air diverted its entire ten-man team away from its main project to focus on Meerkat, which had raised $14 million and was valued at $54 million in its first year.

Unfortunately, as sometimes happens with startups, Meerkat's fall was as dramatic as its rise. It had trouble keeping up with demand, and larger competitors such as Facebook and Twitter entered the market and developed similar products, eventually acquiring the majority of Meerkat users. CEO Ben Rubin realized that, at least for the time being, live streaming was best as a feature on an existing network, not as a stand-alone app. He called together his team to discuss what they'd learned from Meerkat and their previous apps. They brainstormed opportunity areas, best practices, what they had already built, and what customers liked best about their previous apps. They decided to pivot yet again to what eventually became Houseparty.

Cofounded by our friend Sima Sistani and built under a pseudonym, Houseparty quietly built up a following. By sending employees to college campuses to meet with student groups, Houseparty hit 1 million users before publicly announcing itself. By mid-2017, Houseparty was valued at $150 million, had more than 2 million users, and currently has a coveted place as one of the top apps in the Apple Store. Not bad for a rise from the ashes, right?

OUR BIAS FOR "DIVERSIFIED FOCUS"

Life on Air's approach is a great example of what we call *diversified focus*. When we use that term, we're referring to the capacity to be focused on what you think is your best idea, while also being aware of what's changing in the ecosystem and the other opportunities that are presenting themselves. By creating a culture that encouraged its developers to tinker on side projects, Life on Air had a diversified approach, developing internal innovation while working on targeted projects.

Diversifying your focus means that you focus on what you're building but don't tune out the rest of the world. Similar to the way big companies do research and development, you need to pay attention to seemingly tangential businesses, because opportunities and threats come from every angle: from head-on competitors to more fragmented and emerging companies. Through utilizing such a diversified focus, Life on Air lives on.

Another example of a company that maintains a diversified focus well is Google. The Internet giant famously encourages employees to dedicate 20 percent of their time to whatever they think will most benefit the company, regardless of the relevance to their current projects. Some of the products that have come out of this approach are Google News, Gmail, and AdSense. Google has benefited tremendously, both from the new innovations that have come from this dedicated 20 percent and from the fresh perspectives and energy employees have brought back to the core 80 percent of their work. It would have been very easy for Google to become a slow, massive cargo ship. Instead, through the 20 percent time allowance, it's retaining elements of a sailboat strategy, creating new opportunities and innovations through thousands of minisails.

We've seen many instances where new companies have been born out of existing ones or critical transitions have been made that would never have occurred had the founders been steadfast on building what they originally intended. One such example is BevForce. BevForce began as a recruitment business for beverage companies and still does it successfully. However, in its early days, companies perpetually asked it for help recruiting nonsalaried hourly staff. It saw the opportunity and launched a new and successful software business line called Piñata, centered around event-based hourly hires. That made total sense, because BevForce already worked with all the biggest beverage companies, but those companies hire for many more "gig economy" jobs than full-time jobs. BevForce could have easily missed that second line by focusing solely on its original plan.

Maintaining a diversified focus is a balancing act. As a founder, you will find that one of your hardest jobs is to say no. You have to decide every day what you are and are not going to do. We're by no means advocating saying yes to all opportunities—that's an entrepreneur's kiss of death. So how do you know when to stay focused and when to change course? Though each case is inevitably driven by context, we have two practical suggestions: (1) Limit your commitments wherever possible with flexible structures. (2) Think journey more than destination. In other words, prioritize learning over outcomes to limit the risk of any given decision. We dig into both here.

FLEXIBILITY: THE NEW KEY TO STAYING POWER

Most of us have an archetypal picture in our minds of what a strong organization looks like. It's a massive building housing thousands of employees, a recognizable logo and name, and a physical presence in multiple cities. These are no longer the markers of strength. Companies are being disrupted and "unbundled" as never before, and those that want to survive need to be agile.

Founder Flexibility

- *Humility.* Humility is the parent of learning. You can't learn what you think you already know, and humility allows you to learn from anyone or anything. It's the opposite of pride, which has been the demise of many a founder.
- *Open-mindedness.* Having a broad enough vision ensures that you're moving in the right direction but not constrained to a single road.
- *Self-awareness.* Billie Jean King called it "the most important skill to becoming a champion." It is a critical attribute to cultivate: knowing how to read the room, how you are perceived, when to keep pushing, and when you need to change your focus.
- *Patience.* You can't be overly caught up in getting everything right on the first or second try. There's no use being flexible if you're not willing to try different things.

How can you build flexibility into your organization? We think it starts with you, the founder (see the sidebar opposite). Then it cascades alongside the major decisions you make around HR, fund-raising, supply chain management, and more. Across these categories, there are many opportunities to do things in a more flexible way. Though sometimes this appears more expensive, given how fast things can change, we place a massive premium on optionality. Here are some ideas for building and maintaining flexibility in your business.

Create a Variable Cost Structure

Having a fixed cost structure means that incremental revenue drops straight to the bottom line. Meaning that once you make an investment in something, the cost is sunk and all the following revenue is yours. Sounds great, right? Yes, except for when things change. In a heavily fixed-cost structure, you're much worse off in down economies or any time things change materially, such that your initial investment no longer serves you. That's why, as we've mentioned previously, we now advocate a variable cost structure more than we would have in the past.

With a variable cost structure, you have associated costs with every product or service you sell that doesn't have as many economies of scale. But if things start going poorly or you decide to scale an activity back, you're not going to end up upside down. Variable cost structures provide flexibility to adapt and try new things in a way that fixed costs do not. It's the difference between investing in a screen printing press to produce T-shirts versus using a company such as Teespring that allows you to create any T-shirt you want on its platform and sell it via social media while it takes care of the manufacturing and fulfillment. You pay only for what you sell (variable cost) versus the fixed cost of a press.

Take Advantage of Low Unit Manufacturing

Inventory is the opposite of flexibility. One of the classic dilemmas for early-stage companies is the trade-off between larger production runs, in which each unit is cheaper, and smaller production runs, in which less up-front cash is required but the per unit cost is materially higher. Though many physical goods companies face this tough decision, entrepreneurs today have a larger set of low unit manufacturing options, from 3-D printing to outsourced "just-in-time" supply chains. Whenever possible, take advantage of technology advancements that allow you to be more flexible and efficient.

Furthermore, beware of seemingly cheap manufacturing options. Your job is, of course, to always be the best steward of your capital and find the best deals to produce what you need, but we've seen many cases when the cheapest route has ended up being the most expensive as the result of a faulty product, lack of timely delivery, or another reason that costs you flexibility. We're always willing to pay a slight premium to ensure flexibility and reliability.

Raise Funds from the Right Investors

We'll touch on this in more depth later in this chapter, but when, how, and from whom you raise money matters a lot in your ability to change course. Different types of investors have different return thresholds and reporting requirements and require different amounts of your time. Be *very* mindful of which investors are backing *you* and not just a specific product. Inevitably, you may have to change course, and you'll have enough battling to do in the marketplace without fighting with your investors. Avoid wars on multiple fronts.

Hire Flexibly

We touched on this in Switchup 4, but one of the most important places to create flexibility is in how you hire. Start by hiring fewer people than you think you'll need. It's very easy to want to fill every need with a person, especially after raising capital. Rather than hiring eight engineers, can you hire two who will manage six remotely? Try a virtual assistant; there are all sorts of services out there that you can use on a monthly basis. One we really like is Clara. We email her, and she coordinates appointments for us.

Have a High Ambiguity Tolerance

Another key to creating flexibility is your team's ability to tolerate ambiguity. Many, if not most, things in the early days of your business will be unclear and feel amorphous. If the personalities around your table are all ones that need concrete answers in order to function properly, this will constrain you more than is optimal. Seek to have a balanced team in terms of tolerance for confusion, to be able to maintain optimal opportunism.

Integrate Internal Functions

When sales, marketing, and product development are all together as one team, they can more easily consider the lessons each is learning. It makes for nimbler, better-thought-out decisions because all factors are being considered in every decision, rather than in silos. Otherwise, even if your company is super small, it's easy for those functions to operate at cross-purposes.

Create "Velcro Teams" Around an Objective

Convening cross-functional teams to fulfill a particular objective is more effective than creating teams organized around a feature. It's like the difference between reaching a development deadline (objective) and adding a function to an app. Feature-oriented teams have a vested interest in pushing their ideas to justify their existence. Plus, when you're outcome-focused, teams can more easily form and then disperse or reform when a particular project is done or a pivot is needed.

Try the Trojan Horse Play

One flexibility strategy that some companies are employing to test ideas is what we call the Trojan Horse. Using this method, companies find an entry point or a variety of entry points that help build up a customer base. The customer base is like their currency, and they then build a business leveraging that customer base and the insights that they glean. Glassdoor is a perfect example. It's a website where employees and former employees rate their employers, which has attracted 25 million users. What's the real business? Reputation management. It's using the data it's collecting to sell products and services to HR professionals who want to change their companies' Glassdoor profiles. It's probably going to IPO for billions this year.

These days, many companies are selling products as a use case for the platform they're building. Their ultimate goal is to license the software or layer it on other folks' direct-to-consumer businesses. That's another Trojan Horse.

Maintain a "Parking Lot"

Similar to the way big companies do research and development, keep a "possible projects" list of things that you're learning about on the side. These are the ideas that make you think, "Hmm, I want to keep an eye on this." Why? Because one of those ideas might be your next great business or may somehow be incorporated into what you're doing right now. Not everything has to work this minute. Not everything has to pay off right now. You don't always have to know where something will lead. Don't get so obsessed with what you're doing right now that you fail to keep track of your other intuitions.

PRIORITIZE LEARNING OVER OUTCOMES

The second way you maximize success with a diversified focus is to prioritize learning over outcomes. Here's what we mean: Every company places a bet when it makes any major decision. If you go through a rebrand, for instance, you're placing a bet that a new logo, color scheme, or message will have a material impact on your customer acquisition. Why else would you spend the money? Traditionally, companies place such bets, watch them play out, and then call them successes or failures.

We see this as suboptimal and binary, the opposite of a diversified-focus approach, because either you succeed or you don't. Either your bet works or it doesn't. Instead, think about placing bets where you will derive value regardless of the outcome. Get value from the journey as much as from the destination. This is really important: any time you try something new in your business, you probably have an idea of what success will look like. What many entrepreneurs fail to do is spend adequate time setting up their bets so that they provide learning *regardless* of the outcome.

If you set up your initiatives properly, the outcomes actually matter less because you will receive valuable insights that will inform future bets no matter what happens to the current initiative. The key to learning from your bets is understanding the range of potential outcomes and thinking about what each outcome would indicate before you start.

Let's go back to Meerkat to explain this more fully, because you can see a lot about what Life on Air learned from that product, not only in the Houseparty app it created but in how it developed and tested it.

With Meerkat, the company did a huge media push right off the bat that resulted in such demand that the back end couldn't keep up. All eyes were on its every move, and every stumble was public. With Houseparty, it kept the app under wraps (or tried to; eventually someone broke the news of the project) until it had tested and adjusted it enough to be confident that there was a market and the back end could support its customer base. That's learning!

Learning well starts with believing that learning is crucial to your success. We adopted this attitude from our dad, who always talked about being a lifelong learner and staying curious. This is one of the most important traits to cultivate as an entrepreneur. However, such a mind-set is not enough; you must also have the discipline to put systems into place to test and gather what you're learning and develop specific learning approaches. Here are the major insights and practices we've cultivated that we believe will help you as well, things you as an entrepreneur can do.

Develop a Growth Mind-set

Kevin from our M13 team helped us discover the work of Stanford professor Carol Dweck. Her research shows what so many managers intuitively understand: that people are much more likely to reach their potential (and, we would argue, their company's potential) if they have what she calls a "growth mind-set." This is a combination of five factors we see in most successful entrepreneurs we come across:

1. Embracing challenges by saying "Hell, yes!" when told that something is going to be hard.
2. Persisting in the face of setbacks. This doesn't mean blindly hitting their heads against the wall over and over but finding new ways around obstacles, even if that means shutting down and starting over.
3. Believing that if they work hard, they'll get better; that if they work hard enough, they can create excellence—and they do.
4. Seeing errors as simply learning opportunities. Rather than feeling ashamed or embarrassed, they learn from criticism and mistakes.
5. Finding lessons and inspiration from other people's success, rather than feeling threatened.

Which of these five, if any, is true of you? Not everyone has all five, but you can grow the ones you need by being aware of when you think an opposite thought (for instance, "I made a mistake; I'm a failure and should give up") and reminding yourself that it's okay to make a mistake as long as you learn from it.

As Tony Robbins likes to say, "Progress equals happiness." He also taught us to love the word "practice" because it implies that we are always growing—fundamental for entrepreneurs!

Use Data to Fuel Learning

You have to gather data in order to learn. Otherwise, you're just shooting in the dark. We're obsessed with gathering and analyzing data. In later chapters, we'll give you specific examples. Here we want to emphasize the need to use data in four key contexts:

1. **Grow, to understand your customer and/or give yourself a competitive advantage.** The presentation tool Prezi, for instance, used information from customers to focus more on résumés once its directors found out that a large number of users were employing the tool to

create résumés. Still one of the best resources for this is Eric Ries's *The Lean Startup: How Today's Entrepreneurs Use Continuous Innovation to Create Radically Successful Businesses.* He lays out clearly how to test and iterate (refine your product based on what you're learning) in stages. What we learned this year from one of our advisers, M. J. Eng, on a project we were collaborating with him on is there are two goals when spending marketing dollars on social media as a startup: to drive sales and to drive learning. Unfortunately, these goals are usually in conflict with each other because spending for learning means you're not driving your customer acquisition costs as low as possible.

2. **Find out if there is a secondary data play.** For example, Instacart could be one of the biggest data grabs of all time, given that it has comprehensive data on one of the most ubiquitous consumer behaviors: grocery shopping. Those data are incredibly valuable to big consumer packaged goods (CPG) companies, which could change their market strategies and new-product pipelines based on it. Can you turn your data into dollars? The Levo League, a social media site for Millennial women in the workplace, is now selling its insights to companies that want to know how to attract and retain Millennial workers and consumers.

3. **Preserve capital by learning fast.** Often, people do not study data on a granular enough level and therefore miss key insights. For instance, there are such things as unprofitable buyers. In performance marketing, these are easier to spot because you can look at the cost per order of different channels and see where you are upside down. Unprofitable customers are harder to spot in less measurable scenarios, so it's crucial to pay attention to the time, energy, and other resources that you spend getting a customer to purchase. The more you can understand what it costs you to acquire a customer and how much that customer is worth to you in lifetime sales, the better you can build your business to cater to profitable customers. You can also figure out how to make unprofitable customers profitable. We do a deep dive on consumer acquisition cost (CAC) in Switchup 7.

4. **Use data to help you make key decisions, such as whether to pivot and when to ramp up or down.** Gathering as much data as you can to inform the choices you're making is one way to increase your likelihood of making the best decisions under the circumstances. One of the challenges startups have is balancing the need for data with the reality that, at the beginning, their data pool is often so small as to be statistically irrelevant. However, there's a big difference between "statistically relevant" data and data that is relevant to you as a founder. You can find insights by listening to a hundred customers (not a statistically significant number) and letting that quantitative data direct your qualitative research. Use data to inform where you need to go deeper in your quest for understanding. If you think you're seeing a pattern in a hundred-customer data set, have conversations with individual customers to confirm it. Remember, you don't have to make perfect decisions every time—just good ones, faster than your competitors.

Use Both Vertical and Lateral Thinking

Another way to learn as much as possible is to do two types of thinking: vertical and lateral. Vertical thinking is logical, a step-by-step approach that collects information and matches it against existing patterns in our minds: e.g., opening a hotel based on the insight that when travelers need a room for a night, they look for a hotel. Lateral thinking is entirely different and involves viewing something in a new and unusual light to create a whole new pattern: What if, instead of opening a hotel, you redefine the idea of hotel? Vertical thinking, over time, has led to a variety of hotel types and categories. Lateral thinking, on the other hand, is the engine that powers creativity; it's at the heart of all disruptions. This type of thinking is what powered an idea such as Airbnb. In our experience, we've found that the best entrepreneurs are able to do both.

Take Brian Lee, for instance. At LegalZoom and the Honest Company, he has helped create massive businesses by both improving and innovating on the services and products provided in a traditional industry. Brian is very creative and has a lot of great ideas (trust us, he literally has one new business idea per week, at a minimum). However, what makes him unique is his ability to use vertical and lateral thinking to predict where a product or industry could be three to five years in the future and then go there step by step. Baby products companies had previously been sold online, but they had never been marketed in such a fashion, endorsed by a major superstar, or targeted toward Millennial buyers the way the Honest Company does. By thinking about a traditional industry in an unconventional way, Brian was able to see the potential within a space that others weren't thinking about disrupting.

Richard Branson has also had an extremely successful career as both a vertical and a lateral thinker. When he started Virgin Atlantic in 1984, there was not another airline in the world that put the customer experience first. His ability to think both vertically and laterally allowed him to enter an industry in which new companies typically don't survive and find a way to win—through service, interior design, fun advertising, transparency, and, above all else, care for the customer. His ability to think differently also allowed him to launch Virgin Galactic, the spaceline that is set to democratize access to space. As he says, "You don't learn to walk by following rules," meaning that you need to think outside of constraints in order to innovate.

You need both types of thinking to make the most of what you learn from the data you collect, the people you talk with, and the experiences you have. Otherwise, you're likely to jump to conclusions that fit your preexisting patterns and beliefs, resulting in your missing key business opportunities. There are all sorts of resources for creative thinking available that can help you break out of your normal paradigm. One of our favorites is a simple question directed at any idea or belief we hold strongly: If this weren't true, what then?

PUT YOURSELF INTO INTERESTING CROSSHAIRS

A great way to develop a diversified focus is to put yourself into interesting crosshairs. In the previous chapter, we talked about finding the right people to partner with. Here we're talking about casting a wider net so that you develop the kinds of varied and eclectic relationships you need to feed your diversified focus. Who are the people who can give you access to a wide set of information, people, and experiences, and how can you find them?

You start by having some kind of "currency." We discovered by accident that having a spirits company is like having the ultimate currency. How have we been able to cultivate relationships with celebrities and influencers? Originally, they reached out to us to provide liquor at their events, which was great for us because it helped our brand become associated with them. VEEV's success also got us invited to conferences such as the Inc. 5000 Conference, where we got to know the founders of companies such as Pinterest, Ring, and Lyft, all of which we invested in. Then we strategically sought to provide value and make ourselves indispensable in any way we could.

With a little creativity, you can develop your own currency to get into interesting crosshairs. With VEEV, when we started talking to the Walmarts of the world, we excited them with the technology-enabled marketing we were doing—for example, geofences that use GPS beacon technology to determine where you are within a store, then send you store offers based on your location; and mobile apps to drive people to shelf purchases, such as Ibotta. They wanted to talk to us to learn more.

One of our favorite people is Troy Carter, who's a great example of someone who consistently puts himself in interesting crosshairs. For many years, he was Lady Gaga's manager. He's been on the cover of magazines such as *Wired* and a guest judge on *Shark Tank* and is one of the most recognizable tech investors. He and Scooter Braun are two people in LA who've had success in music and subsequently become successful technology investors.

At one point Troy decided to sell his music business to focus exclusively on technology investing but ultimately bought it back after realizing that the music business was a large part of the currency that kept him relevant and so he could take advantage of the technology opportunities that came out of it.

Unlike Troy, too many entrepreneurs get so focused on executing their idea that they don't connect with anyone except folks in their exact space. They think, "I'm starting an orange gadget company, so I have to go to the orange gadget company conference." Of course you want to learn from people who know your territory, but you also want to learn from those outside your industry. It's a way to stimulate lateral thinking. Who knows who will have an insight that you can take from their industry and apply to yours to create a killer combination that no one else has?

You need to be having conversations with generally interesting people to generate new ideas. That's one of the reasons why Courtney is a member of YPO (formerly the Young Presidents' Organization) and why we both are such fans of the Summit Series, which specializes in bringing entrepreneurs together and creating positive change. They've both allowed us to meet people from around the world and deepen relationships with them. Summit's BHAG (big hairy audacious goal) is to be a hybrid of TED and Davos. It's certainly not a small goal, but its first step in doing so is to create a year-round community at Powder Mountain in Eden, Utah. We've spent a lot of time there and plan to spend a lot more in the years to come.

One thing both of us focused on when we moved to LA was creating a list of the people we wanted to know and then setting out to get to know them. Some folks we ended up not liking, and some who weren't on the list have become our best friends. You never know what's going to come from doing this, but we think being deliberate is a good place to start.

Another way to put yourself into interesting crosshairs is to find a coworking situation, such as WeWork. Coworking is like the new post office. We grew up in a small town where people would go to the post office to mingle with their neighbors and find out who was doing what and who needed what. Today, WeWork and the like enable a similar sharing of intelligence.

Under the old entrepreneurial model, you'd go to Starbucks and work by yourself on your laptop with headphones on. These days that person's not very successful. The new entrepreneur is sitting in a crowded room with people all around her. She's working on her laptop and overhears what the guy next to her is doing, and that gives her an idea for what she should do next.

ITERATION AND PIVOTS

This Switchup would not be complete without our thoughts on iteration and pivots, which is how you take what you're learning and change course. Iteration is the cycle of adapting, building upon, or expanding your product or service based on feedback and testing. Typically, with startups, you put out an initial MVP, test the response to it, adjust it based on the feedback, then test again. Rinse and repeat until you have a fully polished product. Each cycle of this product development process is called an iteration. A pivot, on the other hand, is when you decide to change course in what your company is doing (see the sidebar opposite for common pivots).

Successful startups iterate and pivot based on data. They learn from customers and design tests to iterate further. They change directions in a leveraged and calculated way. Iterating, by definition, should be built into your DNA as a startup. One of our favorite examples of a company building testing and iterating into its DNA is *The Huffington Post*. When Arianna Huffington started the publication, one of the things the media site did was produce huge amounts of content each day and then, through their content-management software, watch closely which pieces were shared by readers and then double-down on the clear favorites—creating a viral flywheel. The story that we shared about VEEV at the beginning of this Switchup is another example. While traveling, we observed people mixing vodka and Red Bull, thought about a vitamin-infused concept, learned that that wasn't possible, and eventually developed a "better" way to drink, responded to customer feedback and increased the proof, and made other changes. Unlike VEEV, unsuccessful companies jump from one thing to another without validating with customers what's working or not working.

Three Common Types of Pivots

- *Market segment pivot.* Repurpose your existing product for a new segment of customers. For instance, Study Smart Tutors is a small LA-based company that started by creating materials to train students one-on-one to take the SAT and ACT. Over time, the founder saw that the need was greatest in underserved communities, so he found ways to deliver his training in large classes through programs for underprivileged youth such as Upward Bound. Same materials, different audience, bigger impact.
- *Customer problem pivot.* Solve a different problem for your customers because you realize they have an issue that your product doesn't deal with that has huge potential. A great example of this is Pinterest. In 2009, Tote, a mobile shopping application that connected users with retailers such as Anthropologie, American Apparel, and others, entered the app market to help make shopping more efficient and fun. Tote provided tools to explore products on phones, document and save favorite items, and share lists with friends. Unfortunately, it ran into issues with generating sales, as it failed to make mobile payments easy. The team noticed that it was being used to create large lists of favorites, which people were sharing with friends rather than buying. They pivoted and came out with Pinterest in 2010, solving customers' problem of cataloging, organizing, finding, and sharing inspiration and ideas online.
- *Feature pivot.* Take a feature from your current offering and reorient the company around it. Meerkat and Houseparty are examples. For this to work, you must understand what customers are actually doing with the product you want to reorient to, not what you believe they should do with it.

Here are four practices to keep in mind when considering iterations and pivots.

1. Honor truth more than commitment.

We are paraphrasing a maxim of Gandhi's here, which we apply in our business by making sure that at each decision point we step back and push each other on why we are thinking of doing what we're about to do. We make sure that we're not going forward just because we said we would. Or that we're not doing something just because we said we wouldn't. What does the current data indicate? What data are we looking at? In order to avoid poor decision making, you have to challenge your assumptions, get as much information as you can, argue against your favored position, and be sure to ask, "If we were at the beginning right now, what decision would we make?"

2. Don't pivot just for pivoting's sake.

You need to ensure that you're pivoting to something people really want. Can you use what you already have to test that somehow? Can you do it as a side project, as Meerkat did?

We're doing this with a small company called reBloom, an all-natural, non-habit-forming drink that helps you fall asleep and leaves you feeling rested and refreshed. ReBloom is not a company that will scale by the billions, as some other CPGs will. It's a product in what we believe to be an up-and-coming category, sleep innovation, so we are learning about the space and its consumers. We're using it as a tool for learning so we can scale what we learn to other, bigger projects. For instance, though one may believe that the primary sales channel for reBloom would be at the grocery checkout as an impulse purchase, like an energy shot, through digital testing we have discovered that people want it on a recurring basis to drink nightly as a sleep aid, so it's best sold through e-commerce, where you can set up automatic reorders.

3. Be willing to make tough decisions.

One of the mistakes we see a lot of founders make is failing to act because they don't know which course is best. It's easy to choose between good and better. And although sometimes you can get stuck between two great options, the situation that's most difficult is one in which it's a choice you don't want to have to make, such as whether to lay off people to preserve your runway. What often happens in such situations is that people procrastinate, wasting valuable time and money. That's because, under stress, you can get stuck in the freeze mode of the fight-flight-freeze stress response, which results in immobility or denial. The worst thing is that this response is most likely to happen when the stakes are the highest.

A growth mind-set helps you avoid freezing because it reduces your concern about making mistakes. A tactic we often employ is to remind our team to pay attention to the absolute dollars. What we mean is that it's easy to get hung up on a decision, but when you boil it down, sometimes the choice is worth only a few hundred dollars. Though this may appear to be a significant amount of money, you must think about how that amount relates to the scheme of what you're trying to accomplish. Often it is just a small percentage of something much larger. This is why it's important to know the true value or risk of a decision, so you can know how much time and energy to allocate to it.

Sometimes you find yourself stuck between a rock and a hard place and just don't know what to do. Here's what we've learned to do: realize there's no good choice, and choose the least bad option. Don't wait for a better option to come along. Taking action increases the likelihood of turning your situation around. You can't learn if you do nothing. As the saying goes, "Not every decision has to be an amazing one." But you need to make decisions to keep experimenting. Don't make any critically bad decisions that will sink the ship, but know that if you are treading water or standing still, you're likely going backward.

4. Beware of taking too much money at the very start.

From the outside, when you're capital poor, it can look like heaven to get a huge cash infusion and a crazily large valuation. But we believe that can be one of those "watch what you wish for" situations. It often results in undue pressure on the business because you have to maintain a certain growth rate to keep your investors happy. It's better to have the time to learn, tweak, and validate your model before convincing the big VCs to give you the big bucks. A tech guy we know is in this boat right now. He's attracted a lot of money and attention, but he hasn't even gotten his prototype ready to test. What keeps him up at night? Worrying that he's sold his investors a multimillion-dollar pipe dream.

Testing and iterating are the best things you can do to manage your risk proactively. Through iteration, you break up your massive, audacious goal into many small bites. Take each one as it comes, and stay flexible to make sure that you are building a better company every day.

Last, staying flexible and maintaining a diversified focus is not just reserved for startups. Our former employer, Goldman Sachs, is a great example of a company that leverages its brand and platform to stay in interesting crosshairs, particularly as it relates to the innovation economy. Since Goldman Sachs does not do much startup investing, it would be easy for an institution of its size and scope to start paying attention to companies only when they become relevant to its core businesses. Instead, visionary leaders such as the president and co-COO, David Solomon, have championed programs such as the Builders + Innovators Summit, where the firm brings together some of the most impressive emerging innovators and entrepreneurs in the country, as well as those who have already attained great entrepreneurial success, to share ideas, break through challenges, and grow their networks. In doing so, Goldman Sachs is keeping its finger on the pulse of the next wave of world-changing businesses.

Think Milestones, Not Time: Operational Efficiency

As VCs who started investing while we were running VEEV, we've seen a lot of pitches over the years. Collectively, these have provided a great seat to see how various founders think differently about growing their businesses. What we've realized is that entrepreneurs often think in terms of time—how much runway they have. Time-oriented entrepreneurs say things such as "We're raising a million dollars, which will provide us eighteen months of runway."

Over time, we've become intrigued by milestone-oriented entrepreneurs. When we talk to these folks, we hear things such as "We're raising a million dollars to hire a CMO and reach a CAC of twenty-two dollars on Facebook." The difference may seem to be just a matter of specificity, but we've come to see that they're two different ways of thinking. We believe that the latter leads to a higher likelihood of success.

How come? We all have the same twenty-four hours in a day, so of course we're all constrained by time. It's impossible and irresponsible not to be highly aware of your bank account balance and your fixed costs. That said, having a milestone-focused approach to your business positively impacts how you interact with investors, how you structure your internal processes, and ultimately what you achieve. Put simply, focusing on milestones helps you get better results in less time.

We first heard of this approach from our friend Pat Turpin, an ex–investment banker and the founder of Popchips. One day he was discussing his fund-raising philosophy with Courtney. At one point, Popchips needed to raise and spend a lot of money to fuel its growth, and Pat described how he had framed the conversation to VCs. "They can get scared," he said, when you keep asking for money, especially for a consumer product. He realized that it was important to explain that Popchips wasn't asking for more money because something was wrong but because something had gone incredibly right.

Pat and his team had a clear strategy for the company and concrete milestones they planned to hit. Given the company's uncertain rate of growth, the Popchips team couldn't tell whether their next target was going to take two months, six months, or nine months to hit. They just knew that when a particular milestone was reached, they would need to go to the next phase. That framing—plus a great product, strong leadership, and a well-planned growth strategy—convinced investors to get on board time and again.

Pat's approach made sense to us, and we began to notice other savvy entrepreneurs using milestones not just in pitches to us but throughout their business to drive desired outcomes. In this Switchup, we look at the benefits of the milestones approach, help you identify the right ones, and make sure you're set up to hit them. We apply this principle all the way down to your daily priority list, to ensure that you are focusing on the activities that will get you where you need to go.

MILESTONES SET YOU UP FOR SUCCESS

Milestones are the steps you cross along the way to achieving your long-term goals. They can be easy or challenging, short term or long term, companywide or personal. If set right, they'll keep you and your team focused on what's important, rather than what's urgent. And in a world where everything seems urgent, it's crucial to have mechanisms in place that enable you to focus on the important. Here are two ways a milestone approach is better than a runway one.

- **Milestones leave room for opportunity.** In Switchup 5, we spoke of the need to be flexible so you can evolve your business as consumer needs and wants change. If you're hyperfocused on the amount of cash you have in the bank and how much runway that gives you, every opportunity will be either consciously or subconsciously tainted by the sense of time running out. Running out of runway is of course a very real—the most real—concern of founders, and we're by no means suggesting that you should ignore it. But by focusing on the important milestones you need to hit to prove your concept or make your economic model work, you leave space to do so in creative ways instead of viewing everything through the lens of time.
- **Milestones keep the conversation productive.** With both investors and employees, milestones direct the dialogue to be more substantive. For example, as VCs, when someone tells us the milestones he or she plans to hit with his or her $1 million, we become engaged in a conversation about whether it is the right target, whom we know who might help, and what tactics might be useful, rather than simply wondering "Is that enough money to get you there?" Within your organization, milestones also lead to more productive team dialogue—less "When will this be done?" and more "What are the challenges to accomplishing this?" Milestones also take into account the macro environment, so they can be changed if needed, whereas time-based targets, by definition, are hard to change and the inability to meet them usually implies some real or perceived failure.

CHOOSING THE RIGHT MILESTONES

It's not enough simply to create milestones. To help you focus on results, leave room for opportunities, and keep conversations productive, they need to be relevant, measurable, and, importantly, commercial.

Relevant

Make sure you're choosing goals and objectives that are core to your mission and on your critical path. An example of a critical path milestone is hiring for a specific important position. Carter always reminds our team, as well as our portfolio companies, that if you need to make a hire, it must become one of your top priorities. Until it's done, you're losing ground by spending your time and energy thinking about filling the role and by not having a person getting up to speed in the role. Getting your team into place is a highly relevant and important milestone.

Measurable

By definition, a milestone is a measurable achievement that is made up of a number of smaller measurable, tangible goals. When you set measurable milestones and goals and track progress, it helps ensure that you stay on track without getting distracted.

Although finding product/market fit (PMF) is an important step in the development of your company, it is not a milestone, because it's not measurable. But you can set up a milestone that will indicate whether you are making progress in figuring out your PMF. Maybe it costs you $15 to acquire a customer and you retain each customer for three months on average. Your team decides that an indicator that you've found PMF is when you reach a milestone of a CAC of less than $10 and retain customers for at least six months. In this case, your team would work diligently toward reducing CAC and increasing customer retention. When it reaches a goal of $12.50 CAC, for example, or attains five-month retention, you know you're making progress.

Commercial

Make sure you choose milestones that impact commercial levers in your business. Say you're running a restaurant. Rather than measuring growth by the number of new store openings, focus on the revenue impact of those new store openings (total sales volume).

Often we see entrepreneurs getting caught up in "vanity metrics." Vanity milestones look good but don't necessarily impact the bottom line—or even the top line: 100,000 app downloads, 1 million registered users, page views, numbers of new retail locations. All of those have one thing in common: they don't necessarily lead to increasing revenue. Of course, there are important milestones that don't necessarily lead directly to increasing revenue, such as getting your management team into place. Just don't be fooled by metrics that seem to be associated with increasing revenue but aren't necessarily.

Here are some useful milestones for guiding your business in your earliest days.

- First repeat customer
- First nonpromotional customer
- Your first 100 paying customers/active users
- 100 new users/customers a day
- Getting to a certain CAC for new customers
- Core management team in place
- Hitting a target churn rate
- Achieving a certain customer lifetime value (CLV) threshold

You can also think of your milestones in terms of what you're proving:

- Proof that there is a market (e.g., $1 million annually)
- Proof that you can scale (e.g., to $10 million annually)
- Proof that the market is big (e.g., $20 million–plus)

For some of these, such as CAC and CLV, you may have two different milestones—one for growth mode and one for steady state/ equilibrium.

Remember that the milestones you set for your company will determine your path forward. If you are having trouble thinking through the different milestones you want your company to hit, take a step back and think about companies that you admire and the types of milestones they have achieved. Or sit down with a trusted employee and chart it out together. After all, your employees will be the ones in the trenches working toward them with you.

Funding Itself Isn't a Milestone

Recently, having raised money has become a badge of honor, especially in the tech community. Raising money is hard, and when you attract great investors and a fresh injection of cash, it should be celebrated. But don't confuse it with a milestone. More money in the bank from investors should *help you get to* your next milestone, not *be* your milestone.

MILESTONES AROUND FUND-RAISING

Though getting funding is not a milestone (see the sidebar above), using a milestone approach when you consider fund-raising is critical. The bigger your ultimate vision, the more this matters. It can be daunting to early investors if they know how much money you're going to have to raise to be successful. Imagine if early investors in Uber had heard that the company was planning to raise $8 billion to reach scale. That would have been daunting.

Instead, break down your fund-raising rounds into manageable chunks to get to your next meaningful milestone. Like Pat Turpin of Popchips, when you need more money to take advantage of an opportunity, you can go back to your funders and show how you have hit your milestones and are ready for more. That makes them much more inclined to say yes, because you've proven you can get results that matter.

There's an art to dealing with investors as you move from milestone to milestone. Here are our top tips on the care and feeding of these important partners.

Look for Funders Before You Need Them

Don't wait till you've achieved one milestone to have a conversation with an investor or potential investor. Once you hit the first, you'll likely need the funding to start working toward the next right away. If you have to stop to find the right funders, you're disrupting momentum, wasting time, and potentially losing any advantage you otherwise would have gained.

Keep funders and potential funders in the loop. Don't update people so frequently that they don't see substantial progress, but don't wait until you've hit your goals to say anything. That way you have your backers lined up for your next move, whenever that turns out to be. Good investors always want to show up as late as possible but still right before the party. When you tell your investors you're about to hit a key milestone and there's clear evidence that's the case, they're going to want to climb aboard.

Don't Lie to Your Doctor—or Your Investors

Although at times you may feel the urge to tell your investors a rosy story to keep them happy, remember that they want you to succeed as much as you want to succeed. Good investors are well aware that it's not always smooth sailing and that startups hit many obstacles along the journey. For a moment, let's imagine that you have a bad ankle, but you don't want to tell your doctor. You know it will be inconvenient to run tests and spend time determining if you need surgery, then to get surgery, and so on. What you're essentially doing is delaying the inevitable—either your injury is serious and needs surgery, or you just need ice and rest. Either way, you need to know.

As with a doctor, don't delay the inevitable with your investors. If you have a problem and are up-front about it, they'll help guide you through the tough time. There's no benefit to lying or modifying the truth, because eventually they will find out. And it's possible that they could have helped you fix the problem if you had talked to them in the first place.

Don't Surprise Your Investors

Letting your investors know that "We only have two weeks of runway left" is irresponsible. On the other hand, contacting them only with good news establishes an expectation that is difficult to uphold. The best investor updates we've seen give both good and bad news—outlining challenges as well as successes for each category on a regular basis. Keep your investors well informed so that you maintain a trusting relationship.

Don't Expect Your Investors to Read Everything You Send

We're invested in more than 125 companies, and although we like to check in with them, to read carefully through 125 companies' updates would be a full-time commitment. If you want specific advice, support, or connections, ping or call your investors personally and ask for it. Target your request based on what you know about that investor's expertise and connections. Use your updates as progress reports that investors can digest quickly and easily.

HITTING YOUR MILESTONES

Once you have created your milestones and gotten the money to fund them, it's all about hitting them as fast as you can. This requires not only having a relentless focus on your milestones but moving down from the strategic level to the very tactical issues of how you and your team spend every minute of every day. Here are our tried-and-true ways to do this.

Three Tips for Winning Investors

1. *Show your smarts.* Convince investors that you understand the industry and that you're the person who will execute this idea the best. We invested in Warby Parker because it was an innovative idea with a ton of

potential. We also really believed in the four founders and thought they could figure out how to make it work. Though we didn't foresee a $1 billion valuation, we believed they had the potential to do something revolutionary.

2. *Show your passion.* Don't just tell investors that you believe in an idea—they hear that every day. Show them! Explain *why* you believe in your concept so much. Tell your story, sell your dream, and try to touch their hearts.

3. *Show your business savvy.* You should be able to articulate your strategy, set meaningful milestones, leverage your unfair advantages, and determine what you plan to partner on and/or outsource. Many entrepreneurs are so focused on talking about money that they neglect to sweat the details. Demonstrating this kind of organization and planning from the get-go will help you differentiate yourself from others.

Prioritize

Although creating your milestones is the first step in the right direction, prioritizing them is equally critical. Yes, you may have some that you're particularly excited about, but just as when building a house, you must lay the foundation before you install the roof. We suggest that you lay out all the milestones you've set, then prioritize and organize them chronologically. You may realize that you need to add another goal or two between larger milestones. Or you may see that some of your milestones are less mission critical and so move them to the side. Any outcome from this exercise is great, because you are thinking about how to achieve your milestones efficiently. A good road map template can help. There are lots of them online.

Be Disciplined and Accountable to Your Milestones

Consider the example of our friend with a four-person tech startup whose first milestone was signing up 1,000 customers, at which point more funding would be triggered. He did research and set what he found to be a reasonable goal: acquiring at least twenty customers per day. He planned it like a campaign, setting himself up in the conference room with a script and an assistant to send follow-up emails. He created two thirty-minute "open-office" times, during which employees could come in and ask questions about other aspects of the business. Otherwise, he was on the phone. He guessed it would take him sixty days, but it ended up taking him thirty. That's what disciplined execution fueled by milestone planning can achieve. What equivalent actions can you or your team take?

Make Sure Everybody's Rowing in the Same Direction

You know this problem well: in a startup there are too many things to do. So how can you and your people ensure that you are spending your time as productively as possible on the things that matter most?

Well, first you must be sure that they know what matters. Studies indicate that almost half of midlevel managers cannot articulate the broader company strategy. Everyone who works for or with you, including partners, should be crystal clear about your strategy and the milestones you are working toward. Similarly, it is important that you understand the goals of your partners so you can align on priorities with them.

Second, you need to create an operating system that helps you create that relentless focus on hitting your milestones. A great methodology is described in Gino Wickman's book *Traction: Get a Grip on Your Business*. In it, Wickman acknowledges the existence of "too muchness" and lays out a system for living in a "90-day world," with specific key goals that he calls "rocks" that can be accomplished in three months or less. These are goals that you believe will move the needle the most for your business in that quarter. Depending on what your milestones are, they can be your rocks, like our friend who found 1,000 customers in thirty days. Or if they are larger—say, getting CAC to a certain dollar amount—you may need to break each one down into specific goals that, when accomplished, will roll up to the result you're looking for.

The traction methodology includes holding weekly meetings to check on the status of your rocks and to brainstorm ways to remove any obstacles to their getting done in ninety days or less. This meeting methodology alone is worth looking into. Gone are the long project updates from each person that take up a team's entire day (let's be honest, you're not listening anyway and are using them to catch up on emails). There's a simple green, yellow, red system where you discuss only issues related to projects when there is a problem or potential obstacle and you need to get back on track.

We use this system for our weekly check-ins. We strongly believe that complexity is often the enemy of execution. In keeping with this belief, we have a running list in a Google Sheet of the items we need to discuss, organized by project in order of priority. When we walk through it weekly, we use the traffic light classification to quickly and clearly note the status of a given item. Prioritizing the most important items is essential to running an effective meeting that drives results in a timely fashion.

Vet New Opportunities with Rigor

You're going along focusing on your milestones, and a new opportunity suddenly comes across your desk. You need to decide quickly whether it is a valuable opportunity or a distraction. Is it going to make your most important milestones more achievable or delay them? To make a disciplined decision, rather than just chasing the next new shiny thing, here are some questions to ask yourself and/or your team.

- Can it wait?
- Who on the team will own this and how much time will it take away from current objectives?
- Is the timing right?
- What's the complexity of the partnership? Are the people on the other end of the deal capable of doing their part?

- Who would make it happen? Who will take up the slack if that person focuses on this?
- What are we willing to let go of to do this?
- What is it realistically going to take in terms of time and resources? (Then multiply whatever amount you come up with by three!)

When you make the effort to answer these questions—and any others that occur to you regarding the specifics of the situation—you create the rigor that results in well-thought-out additions and changes to your plans. Beware of the temptation to say yes to everything that crosses your path; the result will be a muddled mess where you are running around doing a lot and accomplishing little. Make sure you are spending your time wisely on achieving key results that will link up to a larger milestone, rather than lots of dispersed activities. Remember what Michael Porter said the essence of a good strategy is: knowing what to say "no" to.

Find Your Antelopes

It's great to have a focus around your milestones in ninety-day increments and to vet new options carefully. But you also have to make sure you are spending each and every day on the things that matter most.

Our friend Tim Ferriss, the author of *The 4-Hour Workweek: Escape 9–5, Live Anywhere, and Join the New Rich*, is one of the world's experts on productivity and efficiency. Check out his website for lots of tools, tips, and tricks: http://fourhourworkweek.com/. One of his techniques for making the most of every day is something he learned from James Carville and Paul Begala's book *Buck Up, Suck Up . . . and Come Back When You Foul Up*. In it, they wrote about an analogy Newt Gingrich used to prioritize his time: lions are capable of eating either mice or antelopes. If a lion spends all day chasing mice, it will starve to death because it will expend more energy chasing mice than it will acquire by eating them. But if the lion catches an antelope, it will sustain all of the pride for several days. So Gingrich would routinely ask himself "Am I hunting antelope or field mice?" when thinking about big projects. Tim takes Gingrich's analogy one step further. Every day, when looking at his to-do list, he asks himself, "Which *one* of these things, if I do it, would render all the rest either easier or completely irrelevant?"—essentially finding his antelope for the day.

Another, less colorful way of thinking about this is to ask yourself throughout the day, "What is the highest and best use of my time right now?" You should always know the answer to this question because that way you will have clear daily priorities and a schedule that focuses on them.

We recommend constant prioritization, or you'll get to the end of the day, the week, or the month and realize you've been in firefighting mode the whole time. As a founder, you can't afford to be putting out fires all day; you need to be working toward that next milestone. Courtney just installed a whiteboard in his house on which he lists his top five business priorities and top five personal priorities. They stay at the top of his mind in every decision he makes about how to spend his time.

Be strategic about when you work on your priorities. We've been told that according to brain science, it's best to do the big, important things at the beginning of the day when your brain is at its maximum strength from resting and eating. Do so before you tackle all the smaller things that must be attended to, such as responding to texts and emails. If you use up your brainpower on minor activities, you won't have it when you try to tackle your big thinking tasks.

Divide Your Schedule into "Managing" and "Making"

We love VC Paul Graham's notion of "Maker's Schedule, Manager's Schedule" regarding efficiency and time management. Here's our translation: Some of what you need to do at work is manage projects and teams, which requires meetings, meetings, and more meetings. Other times, you act as a maker, working by yourself on a creative idea for your product, service, or business. Graham's point is that each of these requires a very different kind of schedule, and unless you optimize for the two, you won't be as productive at either as you could be.

Makers need long periods of uninterrupted time to be in the creative zone to produce great results. Research shows that it takes as long as thirty minutes just to prepare for a new project mentally. Every time you are interrupted by a manager's task, that flow is disturbed and it takes up to another thirty minutes to get back there. That's why so many creatives prefer to work at night; there are fewer interruptions. Managers, on the other hand, live by the calendar, with meeting times slotted into specific increments of time.

As an entrepreneur, you need to do both, which means that you need to plan your schedule very carefully to give yourself time for both. You can't simply block off thirty to sixty minutes for creative thinking in the middle of a day full of meetings and expect good results. It's much better to understand when you need to be in the maker's mode and schedule accordingly. This means:

- Blocking out uninterrupted time on your calendar—consider it a meeting with yourself
- Notifying those who work for and with you that you will be offline
- Turning off any distractions, such as pings and email notifications

Manager mode takes some thought, too. Which works better for you, stacking all your meetings on one day? Or having maker mornings and manager afternoons, so meetings are spread out more or because you need daily stand-up meetings to keep the momentum going? To make this work for everyone, consider having maker days for the whole team, when no meetings are held and you don't expect them to reply to you until the end of the day. Be aware of the different needs of each mode, and schedule accordingly so that you make the best use of your brainpower.

Courtney's Golden Rules for Letting Nothing Slip Through the Cracks

- Pick an organizational system and stick to it 100 percent. Otherwise it's like doing a diet for a week and then complaining it doesn't work. I like David Allen's "Getting Things Done" methodology, which includes categories such as "Next Actions" and "Waiting for Others." "Next Actions" I review daily for things I have to do. The "Waiting for Others" category gets looked at weekly. If I haven't heard back from people, I send a follow-up email. This way, I track each and every important email with a minimum of worry.
- I also do David Allen's "airplane view," where, once a week, I review everything current and coming up from a high view to understand what my priorities should be for the next week, as well as what I need to be thinking about for the future.

Maximize Every Minute

Because time is such a limited resource and speed matters so much, we're obsessed with thinking through how we spend each and every minute. Carter refers to it as "calculating return on invested time"—literally asking yourself, after every activity, what was the return on spending that particular stretch of time? Was it worth it?

Take the concept of opportunity costs and drive it down to each hour of your day. Otherwise, it's too easy to make the classic entrepreneurial error: "It's better for me to do this [drive to the UPS store, manage your inbox, book your own travel, and so on] than to hire someone, because it saves money." This isn't smart thinking. What important things are you not doing when you're spending time on these activities? Every minute you do something meaningless, you are spending a minute you could be using to do something crucial.

We're really serious about this for ourselves. Carter has given up driving and exclusively uses Lyft so he can work while he's in transit. He's been doing it since he realized that driving was costing him an hour and a half each day, which adds up to more than a month per year. Switching to being driven means he gains a month a year over his commuting competitors. It's also one of the reasons we invested in Lyft—we think being driven is the wave of the future, for greater productivity and efficiency.

We also think about opportunity costs in constructing our daily schedules. If we're going to the gym, we book meetings near it before and after. Though holding meetings and calls with everyone we want to meet with would be ideal, we've realized that it's simply impossible. Therefore, we schedule the highest-priority meetings and try to leave the door open for the unexpected encounter that will lead to something great. With practice, we've gotten good at saying, "We'd love to meet with you and wish we had more time, but we probably only have thirty minutes." Then we pick a convenient place to meet. That way, even if nothing comes of the meeting, we've invested only thirty minutes, versus an hour or more.

To analyze where and how you are spending your time, we suggest this four-square exercise (see graph opposite). Divide a paper into four quadrants and go back through your calendar in detail, putting each activity you've done in the last week into one of them. If you haven't kept close track, do so for a week and then try the exercise. Once you have everything sorted into one of the four quadrants, think about how you can maximize your time in the two upper quadrants, eliminate items falling into the lower right one, and find ways to get the things in the lower left done by automation, delivery services, or other people.

THINGS THAT ONLY I CAN DO TOWARD KEY MILESTONES	THINGS I DID THAT ONLY I CAN DO THAT OTHERWISE ADDED GREAT VALUE
CONDUCTED MARKET RESEARCH, WROTE BRANDING STATEMENT	TALKED TO PROSPECTIVE INVESTORS, LED TEAM ALIGNMENT MEETING
THINGS I DID THAT ADDED LITTLE VALUE THAT SOMEONE ELSE COULD DO	THINGS I DID THAT ADDED NO VALUE
CREATED POWERPOINT, SHOPPED FOR SNACKS FOR THE MEETING	DROVE 3 HOURS TO GIVE A TALK FOR 1 HOUR TO A FEW PEOPLE

Check In at Different Levels

Not all meetings are created equal, nor should they all be run the same. Some meetings should be tactical; some should be high level, strategic, and decision oriented; and others should be expansionary or brainstorming sessions. Often meetings are a conflation of all three, and productivity is lost as a result. Having specific meetings for each of these purposes at different time intervals will help you and your personnel drive toward your milestones in unison.

Why Maximizing Every Minute Matters

The Fidget Cube was one of Kickstarter's top-funded projects in history, raising almost $6.5 million. But the company ran into serious design and manufacturing issues. A competitor, Stress Cube, took advantage of its delays to launch a virtually identical product, making almost $350,000 in two months of 2016 over the lucrative holiday season. Meanwhile, some folks waited six months or more for their Fidget Cubes, with promised delivery dates slipping again and again.

Be Efficient in Your Decision Making

Do you end up having meetings in which things are discussed over and over without decisions being made? Total waste of time. To create greater speed, here are three questions you should clarify before a decision-making conversation:

1. How will this decision be made? Consensus is typically the kiss of death for good decision making. It's time-consuming and can totally derail you. Successful founders often use the "get-input-and-then-I-decide" method. Some go around and take a vote. How you do it matters less than articulating it to the group and then using the process you've decided upon.
2. Who needs to contribute input? Does everyone on the team need to be consulted? Whose opinion would be useful?
3. When will we decide? This depends on how important the decision is. It's easy to waste a lot of time talking about decisions that don't matter much. Know in advance how much this matters, and tell your team, "Let's decide this right now." Or "I want us to think about this for a day."

Take Advantage of Productivity Tools

There are literally thousands out there, and more are being added all the time. Here are a few of our current favorites for startups.

- Zapier enables more than 750 apps to work together to automate all kinds of tasks. IFTTT also connects apps together automatically by allowing you to set up a host of "If [this happens], then [do that]" commands.
- Evernote is a great way to track all your thoughts, plans, and assorted info in one place that you can access from all your devices. The best thing about it, from our point of view, is that you can use it to set up David Allen's "Getting Things Done" methodology.

- If you are out there making connections with potential partners and funders, you need something like Humin. It keeps track of your contacts for you, all the way down to where and how you met.
- WorkflowMax is an integrated job management platform that can help you with everything in a small business, from invoicing and costing to client and lead management. They claim they save their clients more than 628 hours per year! Trello, Asana, and Flow are all good, too.

Three Ways to Change Energy as an Entrepreneur (and Hopefully Increase It)

1. Hold walking meetings, and use a treadmill or stand-up desk.
2. Have group stretch breaks, and offer professional massage on demand (we love Soothe for that!).
3. Take advantage of all the healthful food delivery options and healthful snacks out there. Our old friend Sean Kelly, who started SnackNation, can help with this!

YOU HAVE TO HAVE THE STAMINA TO DO THE WORK

Everything is either an investment or a return on investment, so manage your energy, not just your time. That means taking care of yourself—eating and drinking healthfully, exercising, getting enough sleep. We love the work Arianna Huffington and her organization Thrive Global are doing to end the epidemic of stress and burnout. For years, people have been equating burnout with dedication and success. But the culture is shifting, and the science is clear: when we prioritize our well-being and take time to recover, our decision-making, our creativity, our productivity, and our performance dramatically improve across the board.

Pushing past your limits doesn't work well. We once read that when you're overtired and try to make a good decision, you increase the time it takes by up to 500 percent. New research by the International Game Developers Association has found that productivity goes down the longer you work. If you work eight sixty-hour weeks, you've done the same amount of work you could have done in eight forty-hour weeks. A study done at Stanford University says that fifty hours per week is ideal.

You can refresh your brain by stopping for a recharge every two to three hours. The prefrontal cortex is refueled by protein, exercise, rest/sleep, and fun. So have a protein bar, play Nerf basketball in the office, or take a brief walk. You'll return more productive and ready to nail it.

Nail It Before You Scale It: Model Refinement

In the early days of VEEV, our model was "Deepen before you broaden." Because we were forced to self-distribute, we initially homed in on a small number of accounts in a targeted geographical area of LA. Instead of working to acquire as many accounts as possible, we focused on getting our product onto specialty drink/cocktail menus, perfecting staff trainings, and incentivizing bartenders to increase our bottles per account sold—especially at the high-end image accounts. That "tight" initial distribution and expansion approach contrasted to that of most new liquor brands, which generally take the opposite approach by going "an inch deep and a mile wide." In that approach, brands essentially rely on distributors to get their products into the market in the form of hundreds of single-bottle placements.

By intentionally focusing on select markets and submarkets, we were able to refine our operating processes and develop more effective, better nuanced ways of talking about our product, as well as determine how to identify the right next accounts, train bartenders, and drive consumers to try our product. Only after we had made mistakes, iterated, and made our model work well did we decide that it was time to scale.

Though we might not have realized it at the time, we were practicing what's now become a core part of our startup philosophy: nail it before you scale it. By this we mean making sure that you find product/market fit (PMF), have a reasonable consumer acquisition cost (CAC), and have perfected your playbook so all the parts of your operating model are working smoothly before you go big.

Whereas in previous chapters we emphasized the importance of speed in scaling, the one part of building a business that cannot be sped through is finding PMF. As the venture capitalist Marc Andreessen from the well-regarded VC firm Andreessen Horowitz put it, "The life of any startup can be divided into two parts: *before product/market fit* (call this 'BPMF') and *after product/market fit* ('APMF'). When you are BPMF, focus obsessively on getting to product/market fit. Including changing out people, rewriting your product, moving into a different market, telling customers no when you don't want to." When you nail PMF, you've won a major battle, and scaling is then all about refining the economic model and sales, which we'll talk about later in this chapter.

Too often we see leaders who have the entrepreneurial instinct to move quickly go wide before they've nailed the most crucial early steps. Part of this is avoidable by setting, prioritizing, and achieving the milestones we spoke of in Switchup 6. But even with those in place, we still see founders trying to go wide too early. Consumer products businesses fall into this trap when they start entering accounts across the country based on who will take them, rather than focusing on concentrated areas where they can pay the necessary attention to each account. By going wide, these companies are missing the lessons they need to nail their PMF and their operating model by paying close attention to a focused area. Expanding in this random way may result in nonstrategic growth, leaving you with little control of overall strategy to ensure that channels and partnerships are aligned with your brand.

In addition, this type of random growth often includes avoiding markets that don't initially take a liking to your service or product. Though avoiding those potential customers or markets means less rejection, it also means that you'll never learn how to improve your status with them—something you need to explore if you want to scale.

Though we completely understand the urge to expand quickly, even if you are a speedboat, a significant amount of effort should go into perfecting a business before you attempt to grow it widely. By the time we took VEEV to the next level, we had many key lessons under our belts, were confident in our PMF, and had all this energy and enthusiasm that we'd been bottling up during the "nail it" phase. By the time we sold the company, we had a meaningful presence in all fifty US states. We couldn't have scaled the way we did had we not spent the up-front time to properly nail it.

TAKE THE AIRPLANE, NOT THE STAIRS

Here's why working it out before blowing it out matters so much these days. In the past, growing a business was a far more linear process. If you opened a restaurant chain, for instance, you would build one store, then another and another. Growth, as a result, was incremental. We refer to this old way of growing as the "staircase" model. Today, however, market conditions are different and companies can grow exponentially. Doing so requires a different approach.

The chart below is just one indicator of how growth in today's market is accelerating. Notice how CAGR (compound annual growth rate, which measures the year-over-year growth of a company) has increased dramatically for venture-backed startups over the last fifteen years.

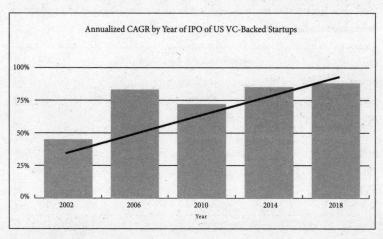

Annualized CAGR by Year of IPO of US VC-Backed Startups

Beyond this chart, the larger market trend that we're seeing is that although startup companies are accelerating their annual growth rates, they are doing so by first perfecting their PMF and operating model and then rapidly accelerating. If in the past healthy growth was similar to climbing a staircase, today you want growth that is closer to taking off in an airplane. Essentially, you have to spend enough energy on the ground building the plane and its momentum so that you can achieve a successful liftoff and start growing vertically.

We're not recommending this approach simply because it worked for us one time. If you follow the business media, you've probably seen a bunch of companies that are in two cities for a while and then suddenly take off like a rocket. It's the operationalization of the speedboat strategy.

Dollar Shave Club is an excellent example. Founded in 2011 by Michael Dubin and Mark Levine, the company became the second-largest razor company in the United States, selling to Unilever for $1 billion in 2016. Note in the chart below how the company's sales were relatively flat for the first couple of years. That was the "nailing it" phase we're referring to in the airplane model, followed by vertical growth, which we refer to as superscaling. Dollar Shave Club used its first year to do what we recommend you, as a founder, do: determine PMF, ensure that your value proposition resonates with customers and that unit economics are sound. Once everything was in place, it was able to take off at an unprecedented speed.

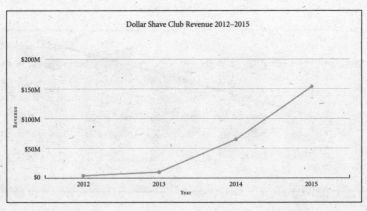

The Honest Company is another example of a business that could have easily been tempted to scale too quickly. Instead, it worked out its operating model and PMF before superscaling successfully. The Honest Company first existed only online, through word of mouth and by leveraging the celebrity power of Jessica Alba. During that initial phase, the management team had the discipline to control its growth and to say no to big-box retailers. They focused on learning what customers wanted and how to source those types of products. That also helped them spend efficiently, as they didn't need to spend money on advertising too early. Once they knew they'd developed killer product lines that consumers loved, they decided to enter Target, where the first purchase order was in the stratosphere. They had perfectly nailed it and were ready to scale.

Without such discipline, it's easy for entrepreneurs to get caught up in a rush and fail as a result of going wide before going deep. One business we recently passed on investing in was a fast casual pizza chain that's like Subway. You say what you want on your pizza, they put it through a machine, and it cooks in just a couple of minutes. It's a hot trend. The business we're thinking of had three stores; one was making money, one was breaking even, and one was too new to tell. The company recently signed a deal to franchise a hundred stores in Canada, with investor backing. We're happy for it and hope that it's a success. But we passed because we didn't believe that the three units were fully baked before they expanded.

On the flip side, there's a New York–based company that we really like, MakeSpace. We admire it because of the rigor with which it tested out its concept, essentially leaving nothing to chance. MakeSpace takes items that you don't often use, stores them, and brings them back to you as needed for a small fee. Although convenient, affordable, well-run storage businesses could be marketable in any city, MakeSpace purposely went deep into specific markets to work out its economic model. Now it has developed enough density in its test cities to drive productive routes and do enough pickups and drop-offs per truck to operate profitably. It also built route management software to ensure that drivers make productive routes and warehouse software for seamless customer requests.

This is the kind of preparation that we think separates success from failure over time and helped MakeSpace close a $30 million round. Though speed is paramount, patience remains an essential virtue!

THE THREE BENEFITS OF NAILING BEFORE SCALING

Here are three of the biggest benefits to using this Switchup—to, as Carter likes to say, "walk, then sprint":

1. You minimize risk.

Although taking a little bit of extra time may sound like a scary undertaking, having the discipline and patience to "nail it" can save you time and money in the long run. We know of a lifestyle startup that ordered 10,000 mattresses once they believed they had enough of a customer base. Three months later, customers started returning the mattresses, feeling that they became less desirable over time. The company hadn't taken the time to get a true PMF. You can bet they wished they'd dug deeper before ordering such a big production run.

As an entrepreneur, you are going to have to take risks. It's a part of the game, but working out the kinks before you go big is a way of mitigating them. You should always be thinking about how to make more educated decisions. The less risk you take on, the more stable the foundation of your company.

2. You create buzz and word of mouth.

Scaling is particularly hard when you don't have brand awareness, yet brand awareness is built through scaling—it's kind of a catch-22. Our approach with VEEV—going slow in the beginning—actually made acquiring customers easier. By saturating one market or submarket at a time, we started building the best marketing channel there is: word of mouth (WOM). We created virality in small pockets, such as Venice Beach, California, and the virality spilled over to the next pocket, Santa Monica.

Typically, marketing dollars are spent in two ways: on awareness building (letting people know your product exists) and conversion (getting them to buy it). That's why WOM marketing is the most efficient marketing channel that exists. There's nothing cheaper or more effective than existing consumers describing your product to new consumers and telling them why they should buy it. Buzz means that people are talking about you and you can spend less to acquire your next customers.

It's very hard to create buzz when you're spread thin. Buzz comes from density, and density comes from having a concentrated target audience. Say you're focused, as we were, on Venice Beach, a submarket of Los Angeles. If you get thousands of customers in Venice Beach, you're going to start creating local buzz. Then you can concentrate your dollars on converting the people who already know about you and spread from there. Think about referral marketing: How can you get people who try your product and like it to tell at least one friend about it?

Interestingly, WOM explains why the "influencer" market has become so prolific. With the rise of social media has come the rise of influencers—minicelebrities with a following specific to an affinity or interest area. Social media has democratized "celebritydom" and in the process created a marketing phenomenon. One influencer platform that's particularly interesting, Influential, has a partnership with the famous supercomputer IBM Watson that helps to deliver demographically, psychographically, and contextually targeted campaigns for brands. Behavioral psychology helps us understand how this works. Whereas over 50 percent of customers report that they question and doubt claims made directly by businesses in advertisements, 92 percent report that they are more willing to trust and act on recommendations from people they know or are familiar with. Leveraging that trust is what WOM and creating buzz are all about.

3. You sell your dream to investors more easily and increase your likelihood of success.

Nailing it before you scale it can change how much you're able to raise from investors and the valuation at which you raise. When entrepreneurs are selling widely from the start and showing us vanity metrics, it's clear that they haven't found PMF and it's a quick pass for us. We'd much rather invest in a company that's serving a much smaller customer base but has deep insights. That's what we want to fund and scale.

Nailing solid fundamentals is crucial because good ongoing business practices offer a greater chance to succeed over the long term. When investment capital flows, companies often find themselves putting extreme growth above all other factors, creating high burn rates. No matter how much capital your company raises, this is a slippery slope. The amount you're spending should not be a result of how much capital you were able to raise but a product of your growth plan and trajectory. That's why we often ask companies, "If we gave you a big check, what would you do with it?" The companies that can't show us how they would scale or perfect their playbooks using the money don't get funding.

It's important to create a sustainable business model with profitable unit economics, regardless of how much you raise. Not only will you be better positioned to grow and survive long term, but you will be better able to attract investors when you need them, especially when money gets tight. VCs like to give money to companies that look like sure bets. If you're disciplined with your dollars, you will be that much more attractive.

TRYING TO GO BIG TOO SOON

This Switchup requires a delicate balance. As we mentioned in Switchup 2, companies that wait too long fail because others beat them to their destination. However, companies that try to go big before working out all the kinks can also run into trouble—a jet plane without enough runway space will not be able to take off properly.

Many companies trying to compete in the highly competitive food delivery service space are finding themselves in this situation. These companies are encountering a variety of issues, such as high waste and food costs and low margins—issues that in theory should have been worked out in their first few cities before expanding. At the same time, they run a risk on the other side of the equation of staying small for too long, allowing competitors to emerge and steal valuable customers and market share.

That's why it's a delicate balance. You need to have a sense of what your plane needs in order to take off successfully but not wait too long to build the "perfect" aircraft, or a bunch of competitive "almost perfect" planes will surely take off before you and leave you on the runway.

A rookie mistake is to become focused too early on big players such as Target, Costco, and Walmart. Yes, they are the big kahunas, and they're tempting. But we've seen plenty of examples of companies receiving initial POs from these retailers and then, when they want to do a full rollout, the products are not ready. Or worse, the company fulfills the test purchase order before its product is fully baked, losing out on the larger opportunity as a result. As we like to say, "The easiest part is getting your product onto the shelf; the hardest part is getting it off the shelf."

Though retailers can be your best friends if your product performs successfully, if your product isn't ready or you aren't prepared to produce large quantities of it, don't rush! If you haven't nailed your product, packaging, manufacturing, shipping, and shelf allure, we suggest that you wait. If things don't go as well as planned, if the big player doesn't sell the numbers it had projected, then it's game over; you've lost that shelf space. But if you test, hone, and perfect so that you're sure the product will fly off the shelf, you might dominate that shelf for years to come!

Unfortunately, we have seen many businesses with significant potential make the mistake of trying to climb in altitude too quickly. One company, for instance, fulfilled its first PO with Target, but not only did the company not get picked up for a longer-term contract because its product wasn't fully baked, but when it calculated all the costs of the paperwork for the drop-shipping, overtime, and rush charges it had paid to make the products in the quantity and time frame it had promised, it lost money on every sale. That company, like many others, was counting on the test run to work—attempting to nail and scale simultaneously.

Yes, it's important to remember how quickly competitors are able to grow and scale. But that does not mean that you need to rush! Take a page from Amazon, which did not begin to grow and expand rapidly until it found its place in the market. As we all know, it started as an online book retailer. Eventually it became the largest Internet-based retailer in the world. Companies that have been the most successful with growth have been able to strike the balance between taking their time to perfect their product and taking the offensive by superscaling in the winner-take-all marketplace.

You increase the likelihood of finding that balance by focusing on PMF through the learning and iterating you've been doing in Switchup 5 and what we like to call a focus on relentless incremental improvements, which we look at in the next Switchup. Here we want to do a deep dive on a crucial other factor you must work out: customer acquisition cost (CAC).

NAILING YOUR CAC

Regardless of your type of business, you're always trying to attract new customers. That costs money. It's not just the dollars you spend on advertising but the cost of product samples, discounts, and other promotions that you must take into account. Though the difference between acquiring a customer at $16 versus $14 may seem small, when you're talking about tens of thousands of customers, those two additional dollars add up quickly. Here's the general rule: *Ensure that your customer acquisition cost (CAC) is lower than your customer lifetime value (CLV). The bigger the difference between the two, the more cash you will have to scale profitably.*

Let's start with a definition of terms: CAC is the amount you spend to make a sale. For example, if you own a taco shop and give away a $2 bag of free chips to attract a customer, your CAC is $2, assuming that the bag of chips was the only device you used to attract that customer. More than likely there were other expenses that would need to be amortized, but we're leaving those out for simplicity's sake.

CLV is the total amount that a customer will spend with you in his or her lifetime as a customer. In this example, let's say this customer will purchase a hundred tacos, and each taco will net you $3. This customer's CLV is $300.

Looking at a more complex example, let's say that in addition to the free bag of chips, you also spend $1,000 on a billboard and use a $1 off code to track how well the billboard attracts customers. If five hundred customers come in with the $1 off code and each spends $20, in addition to taking the $2 bag of chips, your CAC is $5 ($2 for the billboard, $2 for the chips, and $1 off the order). In this scenario, you've acquired five hundred customers at the cost of $5 each. If each customer eats at your restaurant twice, then those customers' CLV is $40, and your CLV-to-CAC ratio is 8. That's a really strong ratio. Any ratio above 4 is considered positive.

Different customers cost different amounts to acquire, depending on the channel they come from. You may have one customer who comes from a billboard you paid for, another from an Instagram ad, and yet another through a friend's referral. The CAC of each is different, as is their CLV. The key is to identify the most efficient acquisition channels through which you can acquire the most profitable customers.

You can focus on reducing CAC, increasing CLV, or both to impact this ratio positively. One example of a company focusing on the

CLV side of the equation is Amazon Prime. With Amazon Prime, you pay $99 per year to get unlimited free shipping. Though offering Prime clearly costs Amazon money, it simultaneously incentivizes customers to buy more items and sign up for other services—enough for Amazon to get back its investment plus a profit. In fact, Amazon launched Prime in 2005, and in 2016, Amazon Prime subscription revenue totaled $6.4 billion. To put the power of Amazon Prime into perspective, research indicates that Prime subscribers spend on average $1,200 per year, compared to $500 per year for nonsubscribers. Thus Amazon has found a way to significantly increase CLV for a large number of users.

Not only do you need tactics to maximize LTV, but as you grow, you must optimize for the right balance between scale and efficiency in your CACs. What do we mean by this? There are various channels for acquiring customers. Some are more efficient but harder to scale—for example, WOM marketing. Consider Coconut Bliss, a small dairy-free frozen dessert company. It has used WOM to distribute more than 2 million pints of product each year, producing more than $5 million in annual revenue. While this strategy has helped it achieve this revenue milestone, in order to take the business to the next level, it will need to find a much more scalable tool. WOM will take it only so far.

On the other hand, Facebook advertising, which is a powerful tool for acquiring customers for many businesses, scales very well. One of the reasons Facebook is so powerful as a CAC strategy is that it has so much information on so many people on its platform. It offers both depth and breadth, a rare and powerful combo.

Calculating CAC

When you are analyzing your CAC, make sure you are doing what is called cohort analysis, meaning, do not look at your customer data set as one complete picture; rather, break the data down into multiple subsets, to provide an insightful analysis. You can sort your customers by channel (where you found them), time of purchase, geography, product type, whether they're a first-time buyer or a repeat customer, and so on. The more ways you can organize and analyze your customer data, the more likely you are to identify useful patterns.

Though you should be measuring CAC at a channel or tactical level, don't lose sight of the bigger picture, as well: your overall CAC. Calculate that by dividing your total marketing expenditure by your total number of customers acquired over a specific period of time. Given the proliferation of devices (smartphones, tablets, PCs, laptops, and so on) and social networks, attribution is cloudier than ever, especially within digital channels. That is why companies use promotional codes, as in the taco example, which we highly recommend. Anything you can do to increase your understanding of where your customers are coming from and what they're spending will help you run your business smarter.

Customer Acquisition Is a Journey, Not a Single Event

When thinking about CAC, always remember that customers go through a journey. Running a campaign may not equate to a healthy CAC when viewed in isolation (it may look expensive), but the same campaign could be assisting sales in other channels by increasing searches, driving visits directly to your site, adding to your customer relationship management (CRM) list, and increasing your retargeting pool. Acquisition costs will vary from channel to channel and tactic to tactic. Each contributes in its own unique way, so always strive to improve CAC by channel rather than hold all channels to a steadfast target CAC.

An important consideration is that different channels may provide diverse benefits to various parts of your overall funnel. Thus, you must look at your portfolio of customer touchpoints and channels, since they are all interconnected. Some channels may be great for driving brand awareness or new prospects, for instance, but be terrible at converting those customers. Others may be very expensive from an awareness standpoint but extremely productive when it comes to retargeting. Some consumers will listen readily to your messaging but are really hard to get to buy—"window shoppers." Others may be harder and more expensive to get into the store, but once they're in, they buy. Some customers may need to see your product three times while window shopping and will then come in (or go home) and buy. It's important to be aware of your overall marketing goals and market across a mix of channels accordingly. If you are measuring success only on the basis of "last click," or the actual conversion to sale, you will overlook important prospecting channels where you can cheaply introduce customers to your brand for later conversion.

Be Aware of the Cost of Keeping Up with the Joneses

In thinking about CAC, it's easy to get caught up in what competitors are doing. This is tricky, because often whatever they're doing will set the floor for you. If they're offering free shipping, for instance, you will have to as well, to stay in the game. In the spirits business, this came in the form of donating alcohol for hot events. If we didn't do it, Bacardi or someone else would sponsor the events, so of course we did tons of them. As important as it is to be aware of competitors, you can erode your profits by overly worrying about what the competition is doing, especially if they can better afford it. If you're concerned with boxing out the competition, keep donating the liquor to the parties. But at some point, you're going to be giving away product when it doesn't actually make sense for the business, because the costs are too high. You have to be thoughtful when you give away product, because whoever has the deepest pockets will eventually win that game. Pay close attention to your return on investment (ROI) on any sponsorship or giveaway.

Selling Versus Experimentation

There are always at least two goals when spending marketing dollars: selling and experimentation. These options are in natural tension with each other, given that we all have limited capital and time. We see many entrepreneurs make the mistake of focusing too much on milking current channels (selling) and not enough on identifying their next channels (experimentation). It's a very easy trap to fall into, because finding a productive sales channel is hard, and when you find one, you want to maximize it. However, the world changes fast these days, and you never know when your best-performing channel is going to be disrupted. We advocate spending at least 20 percent of your marketing budget on experimentation, even if you think you've already found a gold mine.

NOW LET'S TALK ABOUT SCALING IT

Are you trying to create the next Snap Inc., with its massive IPO? Or maybe you are looking for supplemental income to fund your kids' college education? In the beginning of the book, we asked you to consider your end goal, but it's especially important to keep it in mind as you consider your particular version of scaling.

Rather than trying to create the next Slack or Honest Company, perhaps you're more like one of the companies from our TV show, *Hatched*, that we were impressed by: Wild Zora, which offers paleo products, gluten-free meat, and vegetable snacks. The company is run by a husband-and-wife team who originally set out to pass along the company to their children, not grow a massive business to sell. Therefore, they're less focused on getting into every outlet and scaling and are more about creating a sustainable business that can support them over time. As a result, they don't want to take VC money and are funding their growth through their profits.

If your motivation is not a large financial payoff, not scaling is just fine. But if it includes a huge payday, it is likely that you will need to scale. And that means thinking about making the scaling frictionless right off the bat.

By frictionless scaling, we mean creating a product or service that will allow you to reach the size you want as easily as possible. A company we've recently invested in, partially because of its ability to scale quickly with limited friction, is ClassPass, the online marketplace that connects fitness classes and gyms with consumers. As we explained earlier, consumers pay a monthly subscription and can attend a certain number of fitness classes each month. Currently valued at more than $400 million, ClassPass requires very little additional infrastructure to expand into a new city.

ClassPass is a great example not just of a company that has scaled with limited friction but of this overall Switchup. Cofounder Payal Kadakia had attempted twice before to build a business that connected folks to fitness classes. Her first project, Classtivity, was like OpenTable for classes. The problem was that people used it to scout classes, so although Classtivity received tons of page views, it was paid only if people booked through the site. Then she tried selling users ten opportunities to try one new class at a new studio. That didn't work either because, as she discovered, once users found a class they liked, they kept wanting to go back to that one, not try new ones. She took everything she learned about what customers wanted and launched ClassPass, which is now available in thirty-four cities and four countries. That's what we mean by nailing and scaling.

ClassPass's frictionless growth stands in stark contrast with our experience with VEEV. We sold VEEV when we did because we eventually hit a sales plateau. We realized that the spirits business was one of the most difficult industries in which to scale. There was just too much friction, and we realized that in order to grow significantly, we would need a lot more salespeople. On top of that, we weren't allowed to sell directly to consumers and even had trouble shipping to certain states due to liquor laws that date back to before Prohibition.

International expansion? People used to ask us all the time why we didn't expand to other countries. We had requests every week from people in other countries who wanted to buy—including the owner of fifty palaces in Kazakhstan. Despite such opportunities, it would have been an unprofitable investment of time to attempt to build the infrastructure necessary to ship alcohol overseas. There are different legal documents, packaging and labeling requirements, and size of bottle requirements, not to mention hiring salespeople and finding distributors in other countries. In the end, it just made more sense to sell to a global company that already had the necessary infrastructure in place to scale.

After our experiences hitting such roadblocks in growing our business, we're now obsessed with frictionless scaling. What about you? How easy is your business to grow? To scale? Are you doing it in your small town? Could you spread it to a hundred towns? Or are you, for example, selling your product through gift shows? Maybe you have already maxed out your potential by attending every single gift show. Even if you don't want your business to become huge, you should understand your potential limits to growth so you can mitigate against them. If selling your product requires live demos that only you can do, for example, you are going to hit the limit of how much you can sell pretty quickly.

Regardless of the size you want to end up, we advocate two important practices: look at your company from an outside perspective, and implement scalable systems right from the start.

Look at Your Company from an Outside Perspective

Ask yourself, "What happens in my operation when I don't show up?" If the answer is "Not a lot," you don't have systems in place that are ready to scale beyond you. If a restaurant would lose its touch without its maître d', for instance, it would likely not make a good franchise. Another key question to ask yourself is "Is my business prepared for the next step?" Think about if your sales volume tripled—could you fulfill your orders? How much extra work would be required, and would you need to hire more employees or change any technology in order to accommodate? Is there anything you could put in place now that would make doing so easier? One simple thing you can do no matter your size that really helps with scaling is to document all processes in writing. That way you won't lose as much momentum as staff come and go. You will have a playbook ready to share that will make you less dependent on any one individual.

Implement Scalable Systems

From the very beginning, create systems that will work when you change from nailing to scaling. Ensure that you have an expandable supply chain and call center support, and server capacity, so that when you figure out the levers that propel growth, everything will be in place for takeoff. Today you might have only ten calls a day, but you want to know that when you have a thousand, you'll be well prepared.

This is a key reason we're such strong advocates of outsourcing everything except your core business, as we outlined in Switchup 4. That way, you'll be connected to the capacity you need when you need it, rather than building unneeded capacity now. For example, with Amazon Web Services, you buy bandwidth based on what you need. When you're at $1 million, you need only a little bit. When you run a Super Bowl commercial and demand goes through the roof, you buy more.

In addition, make sure that you set up processes that are repeatable. For instance, don't just interview someone yourself. Bring in a junior person so that she can see how you interview someone. This way she can learn from you and eventually do it herself.

Take time to systematize the tasks people do routinely. This is so easy to get wrong. In the heat of the moment, it's easier just to do the task again or do a work-around, rather than putting in the extra time to systematize a fix that will avoid the problem in the future. This is a crucial mistake that, if perpetuated, leads to big scaling problems down the road.

Pinterest is an example of taking this Switchup to heart. It is painstakingly creating a marketplace and system that can scale, going superslow now, in order to ensure that the company will scale when it turns up growth.

1 Percent Better Is 1,000 Percent Better: Relentless Improvement

In one of the seminal events of the Summer Olympic Games, the 100-meter dash, the winner used to break the ribbon when he burst through the finish line. You may have noticed that, in recent years, there's no longer a ribbon. Why? Because the runners are so fast and the races so close that many runners seem to break the ribbon at the same time. Whereas a second or two used to separate first and second places, today all eight runners tend to finish within a second of one another. The difference between going home with gold and leaving with nothing now comes down to hundredths of a second. Today's runners are thinking about how to shave fractions of seconds off their times in order to better compete. How do runners get that hairbreadth advantage? By focusing on minuscule differences, from the way they come out of the blocks to tipping their heads forward at the finish line.

The story for startups in today's world is quite similar. Success is now much more dependent on subtle factors that used to be less pertinent but now make all the difference. This is because, as we've emphasized throughout the book, the startup world has become increasingly competitive. Companies have more ideas, more capital, and more access to resources than ever before. Can you think of a time of greater abundance in which consumers have been able to access more goods and services in such a short amount of time?

As a result, competition between companies across the globe is driving the creation of a larger quantity of higher-quality products and services. Today, even if a company is the first mover or defines a new space, it won't be long before a host of competitors emerge. As companies fight for market share, they offer better and better features to attract customers—hence the emphasis on small differences that can help one product or service stand out. Whereas in the past, much weight would be placed on your business idea, today ideas are a dime a dozen. As our dad used to say, "Ideas are cheap, but execution is dear." He was right; it is high-quality execution resulting in the discovery of important minute differences that allows today's companies to differentiate themselves from the crowd.

In the past, offerings such as convenience and location helped companies differentiate themselves and drove purchase behavior. Today, these differentiating factors are less relevant, because they've become commonplace. Let's say there are three athleisure startups—one in London, one in New York, and one in Boulder, Colorado. Because all of them are competing for the same customers, they offer an awesome product, free shipping, and high-quality customer support. Because they are all offering what used to be seen as major differences, the gap between the top athleisure company and the one that fails is smaller.

In order to beat the competition to consumer attention and share of wallet, your team, your product or service, and your company all have to be so much better than they've ever needed to be. As Carter says to almost every startup founder we meet, there's always been "good," "better," and "best." What's changed is that the difference between them is increasingly defined by smaller factors. As our friend Tim Ferriss said on his podcast, "The little things *are* the big things." These days, many entrepreneurs fail because they underestimate the impact of paying attention to details.

This is why we advocate an approach that we like to call *continuous relentless focus on incremental improvement*. How much of a positive advantage can be created by homing in on the nitty-gritty of small changes? In this Switchup we answer this question and look at how to achieve this advantage through testing, as well as by hiring rigorously and focusing on self-improvement as a leader. We begin with a deeper look into what the magnification of small differences can mean for your business.

THE MAGNIFICATION OF SMALL DIFFERENCES

Imagine two predominantly e-commerce businesses: Business A and Business B. Each has an email subscriber list of 1 million people. Business A has an email open rate (OR) of 10 percent, a click-through rate (CTR) of 3 percent, and a conversion rate (CVR) of 2 percent, all relatively "good" metrics. Business B has 2 percent higher performance across these same metrics: an OR of 12 percent, a CTR of 5 percent, and a CVR of 4 percent. Without looking at the chart below, take a quick guess: What's the sales impact of this 2 percent?

Now look at the chart below. You'll notice that Business A generates 60 sales while Business B yields 240. In other words, the 2 percent higher performance across those three email metrics yields a fourfold difference in sales. That's the magnification of small differences.

Business	Open Rate	Click-Through Rate	Conversion Rate	Total Sales
Business A	10%	3%	2%	60
Business B	12%	5%	4%	240

There are two very important things to understand about this concept. The first is that, although by no means easy, such results based on small improvements are achievable. This is where relentless focus on incremental improvements comes in. The second is that this magnification is especially profound in digital businesses, where traffic is so abundant that small percentage improvements are large in an absolute sense. Let's look at the concept of compounding to get a sense of how this amplification works.

THE POWER OF COMPOUNDING

Returning to our two e-commerce businesses, let's say that a sale is, on average, $100. That would mean that this seemingly insignificant 2 percent increase in conversion for Business B actually creates an additional $18,000 in sales. Think about what it means to have $18,000 more than your competition, all else equal, in your earliest days. Strategically reinvested in marketing, $18,000 could expose your company to millions of qualified prospects, driving even more conversions and generating additional revenue. Over time, through compounding, what appears to be a small difference can create an expanding wedge between you and your competition.

Albert Einstein reportedly called compound interest the most powerful force in the universe. That's because exponential impact comes not only from the growth that occurs on the principal but from what's added to the principal as well. In this case, Business B benefits not only from the revenue generated by the 2 percent increase in conversion but from the further-reaching ripple effects that those customer dollars have on future growth. The new customers may share the brand with friends through WOM, generating more awareness, new customers, and even more revenue. As you can see, this cycle is self-reinforcing, so what initially was a 2 percent difference very quickly becomes a serious advantage in further growth.

Why is this so important? Because *all repeated actions compound*, meaning that when you have extra budget because you drove sales through a strong marketing campaign, you're able to leverage lessons learned from the campaign and the extra budget, compounding your sales growth positively. The same can happen negatively. When things are not going well and you need to cut your budget, your drop in spending lowers your brand awareness, raises your CAC, and makes each dollar go less far. Remain hyperaware of the power of compounding in your business. Mistakes compound, too!

A CULTURE OF RELENTLESS IMPROVEMENT

Now that you appreciate the forces of compounding, let's look at how to create them through a culture of relentless improvement. When we say relentless, we mean developing an obsession with making every part of your business better every day. When we talk to business moguls and titans of industry, it is this never-halting search for better that's omnipresent.

Relentless improvement is not an action item; it is a fundamental part of your culture that starts from the top. You help create it by rolling up your sleeves, paying extra attention to detail, holding your team, suppliers, and investors to the same standards, and ingraining this approach in your company's everyday work flow. More specifically, there are three crucial disciplines you need to put into place to foster a culture of relentless improvement. We start with one focused on your business, then move on to one for your team, and end with one for you as a leader.

1. Your business: Test, test, test.

Why should you spend money and time testing? The answer is that testing helps reveal and improve your weakest links, and in a startup, the weak links are what can lead to its demise. Every quarter is an opportunity to set out a series of bets that you will test for approximately ninety days. We find that assessing these tests at the end of each quarter helps create subsequent tests in the next quarter that will help you build on what you've learned, getting better and better in a disciplined fashion. This means setting aside some portion of your company's revenue for testing.

If you're running an e-commerce business and successfully drive traffic to your website but convert poorly, you should be testing what's working to iterate and determine ways to convert better. But you shouldn't focus only on what is working—staying in the "safe zone." It is also important to test "on the margins." This means, for instance, not only testing the color of your landing page but fully testing your brand positioning to see which version is resonating best with customers.

Often there's no one answer to getting 2 percent better open, click-through, and conversion rates. Instead, it's about testing different parts of the funnel, finding small insights, and then scaling those insights so they add up to 2 percent better. Testing the creative, the pricing, where the traffic is coming from—not just once until you find a win but over and over and over again. That's how you strengthen your weakest links and find the tiny differentiators that matter so much these days. Because most major corporations have not risen to success in today's world, they often ignore or are late to the practice of constantly testing. That is why many slower-moving corporations, which are notoriously bad at testing, have been disrupted by young companies that are gleaning insights and constantly improving their businesses.

Equip Your Company to Test Successfully

Tests don't run themselves. You must assemble the right type of team and make sure they understand the importance of testing and how it aligns with the overall company strategy. Here are some roles you should consider in website testing.

- **The owner: Who's in charge of the testing process?** The owner manages the various aspects of the testing process: test design, test planning, overseeing executional support, scheduling, aligning with business executives, evaluating results, and implementing winning variables. Think of him or her as the quarterback of the testing team.
- **Executional support: Who designs creative variations and handles the implementation?** The owner should have dedicated design and development resources. These could be full-time employees or a dedicated allocation of hours per week from a shared resource that has the ability to implement tests quickly and on a regular cadence so they don't end up at the bottom of the prioritization list. Often, tests involve some form of creative and front-end web development and sometimes back-end developers. The designer is responsible for creating alternative variations with guidance from the owner. The developer is responsible for implementing the code needed to facilitate the test.

- **Data science/analytics: Who digests the test's output?** The analyst is consulted during the test design phase to ensure that appropriate events are tracked and variables are isolated so that clean data is generated. During a test, the analyst keeps an eye on performance and collects enough data to avoid making hasty decisions. However, the analyst should also be able to recommend killing a test if its performance is far from an acceptable threshold. At the conclusion of a test, the analyst summarizes the test results and works with the owner to develop appropriate recommendations.

TEST, DON'T GUESS

Plenty of startups make this mistake. We can't tell you how many times we've seen entrepreneurs go through a website refresh or implement new packaging that ultimately led to less of an impact than what they originally had in place because they had done insufficient testing—or none at all.

These days, entrepreneurs don't necessarily know the product mix or sales channels that will be the most successful. That is why you see so much experimentation in the market. There's no one-size-fits-all anymore, no perfect formula for product offering, for business model, for tech platform, for marketing and advertising, for customer acquisition. Each company has a unique takeoff path. You see this in the market today, as e-commerce companies experiment with bricks and mortar and vice versa. Take Warby Parker, for example. It was originally an e-commerce glasses business and strategically tested the idea of opening a small-format brick-and-mortar test store. The test was so successful that it has now opened thirty-one locations and is on its way to fifty by the end of 2017. Similarly, retailers such as Walmart are beginning to develop and test own-branded products. The point is, since you don't know what is going to work best, you need to think about tests that will help you learn what will move the needle for you before you make a commitment of time and money in any direction.

TEST STRATEGICALLY

By definition, startups are organizations built for learning. Sometimes they learn quickly and can capitalize on the opportunity. Other times they learn while struggling and bounce back based on new insights. This is where strategic experimentation comes into play. For example, a friend of ours was launching a social media platform around music. Instead of spending a bunch of money on building a particular landing page, he decided to test which of two website landing page layouts fit the brand better. Prelaunch, he put two very different ones out in the market, directed the customer traffic to them randomly, and looked at things such as time spent on the page and whether people provided their email addresses for follow-up. From the get-go, he was obsessed with listening to customers and improving his offering based on what he heard.

You can gain insights through testing by setting up a series of experiments, or bets, that utilize the fundamentals of the scientific method. That's what we're doing with a number of the projects we are working on at M13. Given that we invest a lot in consumer products businesses, we're always interested to know what customer acquisition tactics are working so that we can share what we've learned with our portfolio of companies. We do this by paying attention to investor updates and by digging into the strategies and best practices of top performers. We also do it by owning and operating our own "test brands."

For instance, we bought a brand called Sole Serum. It's a very small e-commerce company that sells a serum to help reduce foot pain, especially for women who wear high heels. The brand is sold only online. Together with our partner Innovation Department, we are running strategic tests to determine the best channels for acquiring email addresses. We're also testing a variety of shoppable video software platforms. These low-cost tests provide learning that is not always directly replicable in other companies but can set us in the right direction and help save time and capital.

Because time is your greatest asset, you should ensure that your tests have the potential to answer important questions or yield impactful insights. Utilizing the steps of the scientific method will help you do testing that yields useful results.

1. **Make an observation.** For instance, take note that a certain channel is leading to a higher average order value (AOV) compared to other channels.
2. **Ask a question.** What's causing this group of customers or channel to spend more? How might we use what we've learned from this channel to raise AOV on other channels?
3. **Form a hypothesis.** These customers are spending more in response to a specific type of messaging on a specific channel, so that same type of messaging can be further leveraged across the company.
4. **Conduct an experiment.** Set up a baseline (regular messaging) and then a few variations of messaging, including the type that you want to test.
5. **Analyze the data.** Collect results, and think about the different messaging responses. How does this information confirm, deny, or redirect your initial hypothesis?
6. **Draw a conclusion.** Think about how the answer to your question or experiment is applicable to the broader company and how the insights gleaned from the test will be useful in the future.
7. **Implement a change.** Based on the results, implement the winning message. Be sure to measure results post-implementation to ensure that performance improvements are maintained.
8. **Rinse and repeat.** Continue to find ways to improve performance by trying to beat your new baseline.

Don't Test in a Vacuum

Keep in mind that when testing one thing, you are more than likely impacting something else simultaneously. For example, say you were trying to improve the click-through rate of an email campaign. Perhaps you used a salacious image or made some superlative claim; you might succeed in increasing the number of users who click through and visit your website. However, you haven't necessarily increased sales. If sales remain flat despite the improved response rate, you've inadvertently reduced your site's conversion rate by driving a high number of unqualified visits to the website, with no incremental sales.

Interactions aren't always negative. We've seen positive results spill over to other metrics. While helping grow the brand awareness of one of our partners, we found after a series of tests, including a collaborative sweepstakes, that we were not only encouraging people to follow the brand on social media (the intended effect) but also growing its customer relationship management (CRM) list. When conducting your tests and analyzing the results, be sure to step back and look at the whole picture. As our dad used to say, "What affects one thing directly almost always affects everything else indirectly."

BE PROACTIVE, NOT REACTIVE

Instead of waiting for insights or observations to come to you, seek them out early and in advance. For instance, while working on creating VitaFrute, our organic ready-to-drink product, we saw the emergence of Bethenny Frankel's Skinnygirl Margarita product, and we knew that we had two options: either we could sit back and watch to see whether it took off before we took action—the reactive approach—or we could immediately start testing and leveraging digital and social media in order to determine how we could compete—the active approach. We already had the product in place, so we tested words such as "skinny," "natural," "organic," "better," and others, in order to see which resonated best with consumers and which would compete best with products such as Skinnygirl.

If we'd taken VitaFrute straight to the shelves without doing such testing, we would have had to wait to see the answer and maybe lost our chance to compete. But by testing immediately, we were able to narrow down to the best way to advertise our product and were confident that we selected the best strategy while also helping create a new category.

WHAT TO TEST

Following are some specific tests that are especially relevant for e-commerce businesses, but they can also be applied to offline busi-

nesses. The point is to test highly targeted parts of your consumer funnel, so you can understand where the leaks are as you build.

- **Landing page.** Most people think of adding callouts, images, additional text, and reviews to their website. Try removing elements
  one at a time and seeing how that changes user engagement and
  sales. You may be surprised at how well consumers respond to less
  when they're always surrounded by more. What are the clickable
  parts of your site? How intuitive are they? Experiment with different buttons by changing the color, the word within the button, or
  the placement. Especially when you've visited your site hundreds
  of times, you may be conditioned as to where everything is, so test
  your calls to action to make sure people aren't missing them. What
  content are you using on your site? Is it branded, user-generated,
  animated? Is it product-centric or lifestyle focused? All of these
  factors should be tested until you know what works.
- **Cart checkout.** What information are you asking for at checkout?
  Do you need *all* of it? Are you going to do anything with it? Do
  you know how many people are adding items to their cart and
  not checking out? What would you be willing to forgo in terms
  of information if by so doing you could increase your sales? What
  payment options are you currently not accepting? Do you know
  how much that is costing you?
- **Email subject line.** What does your current subject line say or do,
  and what is your customer looking for? What are competitors putting into their subject lines? One at a time, focus on testing tone,
  word count, and punctuation.
- **Creative.** What ad formats are you using? Static image, animation,
  native, and/or video? Are you testing the same content in different
  formats to see which performs best? How about calls to action: Are
  you testing "Buy now" versus "Shop now" versus "Learn more"?
  How about testing ad sizes and placements? You'd be amazed by
  how subtle changes can make big differences!
- **Discounts and promotions.** What kinds of promotions have you

tried? Do you know what kinds of incremental sales you get when you offer 15 percent off versus 10 percent? What's your optimal balance between running promotions and maintaining your margins? What about shipping—have you seen how free shipping affects your sales? How does a certain percentage off compare to an extra service such as buy one, get one free or a coupon offer for a friend?

2. Your team: Hire the right people.

In addition to rigorous testing, one of the best moves you can make toward creating a culture of relentless incremental improvement is to hire the right people. This means understanding your business and the roles you are looking to fill. Although hiring amazing people is important, hiring based on fit is equally important and often overlooked by founders. We like to think about this in terms of former basketball coach Phil Jackson's "triangle offense." Using that strategy, Jackson found that some of the best athletes were not necessarily the right players to fit into the system. It didn't mean that they weren't great players; they just weren't right for the job. What kind of offense are you running, and what kinds of players fit into it?

In addition to hiring people who fit the company, you must find great people. What do we mean by "great" people? One thing we like to avoid is employees who have an "employee" mind-set instead of an "ownership-building" mind-set. They're there to collect a paycheck, as opposed to being interested in building the organization with you.

Bastian Lehmann, the CEO and cofounder of San Francisco–based Postmates, recently underscored the importance of this approach. When asked what he would do differently if he had a do-over, he replied, "Even though I spent a large amount of my time on recruiting, and we understood how important it is to have the right people do the right jobs, I think we underestimated how a couple of extra people can change the outcome of a company. . . . The impact of a couple of people is dramatic."

We vehemently agree, with one obvious addition: it depends on the quality of the people. Without a doubt, hiring great people is the hardest, yet most rewarding thing that every entrepreneur does. It's time consuming and not easy to get right—we've all made memorable mistakes. And those mistakes are expensive—according to Geoff Smart, a coauthor of *Who: The A Method for Hiring*, a single hiring mistake costs fifteen times base salary in hard costs and productivity loss.

Avoid the "Too Good to Fire, Too Bad to Keep" Mind-set

More than the cost of time and money involved in hiring the wrong person, the true cost to a startup comes from mediocre team members. If someone is really bad, it's easy to let him or her go. But if he or she is mediocre, you tend to keep him or her around too long. In a small startup, you simply can't afford a 5- or 6-out-of-10 performer.

Startups are like what we call a "weak-link sport"—a game in which the progress of a team is limited by its weakest performer. Unlike basketball, a strong-link sport in which a team can dominate with one superstar player, soccer is a weak-link sport. Because it's so team oriented, a team is only as good as its weakest player. For instance, Germany won the last World Cup with fewer stars than some other sides had because its tenth- and eleventh-best guys were a lot better than those on other teams. Germany had no weakness to exploit, and for that reason, other teams had trouble scoring on it—it was unbeatable.

Startups can easily fall victim to the weak-link effect. As a leader, you must develop the rigor to hire the best you can in the first place and the will to admit when a particular person isn't good enough and must go. The more competitive the startup industry is, the more important it is to avoid having a weak link.

This is especially true when you are first launching and can spread responsibility among very few employees. We find that hiring one well-rounded person who has competencies and experience in key areas of what you are doing is a better choice, option permitting, than hiring three people who each do a more specialized task. It costs less, is easier to manage, and allows for flexibility. A metaphor that one of our team members uses is rugby: in certain positions of rugby, the key is to be stronger than anyone who's faster than you and faster than anyone who's stronger than you. We think this is the type of thinking one should use when hiring: look for the best athlete who can handle any number of roles. Especially with a small team, you can't underestimate the variety of challenges that will come up, and therefore, how quickly an employee can learn is his or her most important attribute.

Once you're growing, of course you'll need to hire a variety of people who specialize in particular areas. At that stage, our favorite resource for creating an excellent team is the book *Who*. The authors, Geoff Smart and Randy Street, help you create a hiring process in which you are able to identify the strategic purpose of the role, the key measurable results the employee must achieve, and the core competencies required to achieve those results.

As an entrepreneur, you need to remember that the employees who help you get from point A to point B are not necessarily the same ones who can help you get from point B to point C. For example, when you start a company and are thinking about marketing, you want to find someone who knows the nitty-gritty and can help out with marketing tactics in the trenches. However, once your company is larger and growing, your ideal CMO understands higher-level strategy and knows how to handle big budgets.

FIVE KEY HIRING LESSONS WE'VE LEARNED ALONG THE WAY

- **Ask talented people for referrals.**
  In order to find great people, ask the most talented people you know for referrals. As your company grows, build a referral culture by rewarding those who refer a successful candidate. A rule of thumb we've heard is $2,000 to $5,000 after the new employee has remained with the company for ninety days.
- **Use hiring platforms.**
  If your referral pool is small, take a look at ZipRecruiter, Angel-List, LinkedIn, GitHub, and other platforms to access a massive pool of talented people. We like GitHub because you can see not only people's profiles but also projects they've worked on.

- **Check references and dig deep.**
  Most people use references as a "check the box" activity at the
  end of the process. That's *not* our approach. Dad taught us to use
  references to guide and inform our hiring process. There's no tool
  more powerful in evaluating candidates than the reference check.
  It begins when you ask the candidate for references. How many
  do they provide, and how readily? Are they peers, superiors, or
  personal references?

  When you are speaking to the reference, seek to understand
  how successful the person was in the context the reference knows
  about. Ask: How would you describe this one person in two
  words? What caused him or her to be successful? What behaviors,
  habits, or tendencies limited his or her success? What would you
  surround this person with to help make him or her successful?
  (Some people require a lot of autonomy to produce. Others require
  more structure and direction.)

  Pay close attention to the answers. Tone, hesitations, pauses,
  and enthusiasm are as important as content. For managerial hires,
  we recommend doing reference checks in person, so as not to miss
  any indicators. By digging deep with people who have worked
  with, for, above, and around a candidate, we get a clearer picture of
  a person. This is one of the keys to our hiring process.

- **Utilize personality assessment tools and software.**
  At M13, we ask every serious candidate to participate in a Predic-
  tive Index (PI) test. The PI is one of many personality tests that
  can help you understand what drives a candidate and how he or she
  will work with others. We believe that PIs are important and useful
  because they can help you evaluate how individuals will work in
  your environment and fit into your system. This is particularly
  useful for small companies that don't have an HR team and can't
  afford to hire the wrong person. Imagine that you are looking for
  someone who can work well independently, but the PI indicates
  that a certain applicant needs a lot of direction or prefers to work in

groups—that is the type of insight the PI test can provide you with. If possible, we like doing personality tests before we do reference checks and certainly before final interviews so we can inform our conversations with additional data points. It is important to note that we do not see PIs as replacements for interviews. In fact, we think in-person interviews are the most efficient way of evaluating a candidate. Interviews give you the opportunity to focus on the minor details. For example, was the candidate respectful to your assistant and was he or she on time?

New data by Wharton professor Adam Grant has demonstrated that being a "giver" vs. a "taker" is increasingly something important to watch out for when hiring.

- **Use a try-before-you-buy period.**
In addition to the formal interview process, we believe in out-of-the-office "interview" activities. This is because it is important to see how a candidate interacts in a variety of social settings. Sometimes we take a possible hire out to a crowded restaurant to see how he or she behaves.

Once a candidate is hired, ninety days is typically enough time to see if he or she is a good fit with your team and company. In many roles it takes time to acclimate, but if people have not proven themselves highly valuable to you within the first ninety days, it's worth seriously questioning if they're right for the role. To set the person up for success, make sure you provide clear expectations and make agreements around those expectations. Additionally, set up thirty-, sixty-, and ninety-day goals with frequent check-ins. Many entrepreneurs struggle with the question "Do I need this role in my company?" We find that the best way to test this is with a contractor. After thirty, sixty, or ninety days, you will likely know the answer to your question and can take action from there.

3. Relentlessly improve yourself.

A focus on relentless incremental improvement includes you as a leader. We're great believers in the adage "The way you do anything is the way you do everything." Who you are as a person will inevitably show up in how you do business and how your business performs. If your financial house is not in order in your personal life, for instance, don't expect it to be in your professional life. Hire for that.

To improve yourself in order to improve your business, consider the following questions: What are your weaknesses, and how are they reflected in the business? Where in your life do you need to create greater personal excellence that will drive organizational excellence? How can incremental improvements apply to you personally? Then make a specific plan to develop the qualities you believe will help you drive the success you desire.

In addition to making a self-improvement plan, we'd like to suggest three practices that we've found to be crucial in self-improvement: stay humble and hungry, cultivate the right connections, and do reverse mentoring.

STAY HUMBLE, STAY HUNGRY

When we talk to entrepreneurs we admire who are ten, fifteen, or twenty years older than we are, we're amazed that despite the fact that they've made fortunes and don't need to work anymore, they still hustle. They're still in it to win it. To paraphrase Under Armour founder Kevin Plank's favorite quote, they "stay humble and hungry." That's why they continue to create phenomenal businesses.

The minute you stop thinking it's all about the hustle is when you no longer strive for excellence. The minute you're not humble and think you know everything, the minute you're not hungry and therefore don't work so hard, the minute you don't learn like crazy from what other people are doing, you set a course to mediocrity and weaken your chances of success. When you're humble, you know you don't know everything and therefore work hard to get better.

CULTIVATE THE RIGHT CONNECTIONS

A key way to improve relentlessly is by surrounding yourself with the right people who can help push you. That's a reason why Courtney's in YPO and why we both go to Inc.'s entrepreneurial conferences—to put ourselves into environments where we can learn from other successful entrepreneurs. The right connections not only can get you to the person you need for a key insight but may help you think about how to do a tiny tweak to your brand that will significantly increase sales. Expertise matters, so you need to be out there connecting a lot. But not just for the sake of collecting names—we want you to be strategic about your connections.

We're not fans of networking for the sake of networking. It's just too time-consuming. Regardless of how many "friends" one has on Facebook, we're believers in Dunbar's number. That's a concept created in the 1990s by Robin Dunbar, who maintained that, based on how our brains are structured, there is a 150-person limit to the number of people with whom we can have a meaningful social relationship.

We try to adhere to Dunbar's theory by focusing on strengthening a small number of relationships we believe are important. You may want to write out the different types of relationships you have, then think about which to prioritize. Which connections are more meaningful to you? Whom do you know who is well connected in your industry? When you go to a conference, whom would you most like to meet, and how can you collaborate with or learn from that person?

A professional we know discovered that every single one of her referrals could be traced back to a single client. Rather than doing scattershot marketing, she worked on getting closer to that person, as well as identifying other key referrers—people who would send several clients to her. As a result of that exercise, today she is always busy. We want you to be equally strategic about finding and nurturing the right connections.

REVERSE MENTORING

In the past, mentorship worked in one direction: an older, more experienced person helped the younger, less experienced one. In the world we live in now, there's still a lot a 55-year-old can teach a 27-year-old. But there are also things that a 27-year-old can teach a 55-year-old. We saw a deck the other day about where innovations increasingly come from. The vast majority, especially in technology, are coming from people under 30, many of them between 19 and 24. That's why, in tech startups, you so often see a very young tech leader and an older, more experienced business person partnering. Or at least once VCs come in and push you in that direction. Think Mark Zuckerberg and Sheryl Sandberg.

Five Tips for Successful Meeting Follow-up

Our dad liked to say that business is 10 percent about what happens and 90 percent about how you follow up on it. We agree. Here are our five top tips.

1. When you meet someone face-to-face, particularly a well-known person, never leave the conversation without getting the person's personal email address by offering to send them something. Use what you know about their concerns: "Please give me your e-mail, and I'll send you that great article on AI we were just talking about."

2. Find ways to make yourself indispensable. Often, the first impression is all you get. Meeting a potential investor whose son is applying to colleges? Make an introduction to an alumnus you know. Or maybe you attended the school and can speak with him or her about your experience.

3. It's up to you to follow up. Use whatever mode you can to get a response: call, FedEx (some CEOs still open their own FedEx boxes), email again. If one mode doesn't work, switch to another. Never take it personally when someone doesn't respond to your email. You probably just got lost in his mountains of email. If you take it as a sign he's not interested, you'll give up too soon.

4. Be pleasantly persistent. The key word here is *pleasantly*. In our experience, if you're persistent without the pleasant part, you're going to have a high likelihood of rubbing the person the wrong way. Two unreturned emails isn't reason enough to give up, especially when you are dealing with busy executives.

5. Do some research and find out who an executive's assistant is. How can you get to know that person? An assistant can be either a huge blocker or an enabling connection. Treating assistants well is important.

Increasing the Odds That Your Email Will Be Read by the Right Person

Because we live in such an open-sourced, information-based world, it's easy to get anyone's email address, including Tim Cook's. But getting Tim Cook to reply? That's where it gets harder. We love the story of 22-year-old entrepreneur Brian Wong, who cold emailed the CEO of American Express, which ultimately led to American Express's investing in Brian's company. Dissecting his email as well as those of others who've successfully done similar things, here's what we've learned about how to stand out.

- *Be targeted.* Determine why the person and/or company might be right for what you are doing, and write about that. What's the unique selling proposition for the other party?
- *Be relevant.* Offer something the person would be interested in. Brian offered to trade insights on the rise of gaming and "how a reward layer will rule the world, and it might not be ruled by American Express." You can imagine how a statement like that might get the CEO's attention.
- *Be grateful.* A study done by Boomerang found that emails ending with "Thanking you in advance" get a 65.7 response rate and "Thank you" a 56.9 percent response rate, as opposed to standard endings such as "Sincerely" and "Best wishes."

You can take advantage of this, no matter what business you are in. For instance, if you are a 35-year-old stay-at-home mom with a growing business on Etsy, maybe your daughter's high school friend can help you tweak your social media sales campaign.

If you're young, don't assume you don't have anything to offer. See the sidebar above. We imagine that the CEO of American Express, Ken Chenault, was at least as interested in what he could learn from Brian Wong as what he could teach him, which is the real reason he said yes.

More and more people are seeking this type of cross-pollination, to discover what they can do to tweak what they are doing. A good example is the PTTOW! Summit, a conference of the 250 best marketers in the country. All the big hitters from the hottest companies attend. It used to conduct a "blind date" event, where people would be paired up with people they wanted to meet. Of course everyone wanted to meet the same few people—someone from Uber, GE, GM, etc.

So the conference came up with an idea called Brain Date, where they were paired by what they knew and what they wanted to learn, rather than by who they were. It was wildly successful, because people learned a lot from folks they wouldn't have otherwise selected. That's where Carter met the executive vice president of Fossil Group, Greg McKelvey, which led to a collaboration with M13. "He would never have pegged me, the former peddler of booze, as a person he wanted to be paired with," admits Carter. "But because we were paired, we both ended up feeling like we learned a lot, which led to us visiting their headquarters for a follow-up conversation."

Remember, experienced folks can learn from you as much as you can learn from them, so never be afraid to reach out. And be sure to keep putting yourself in the types of situations where you can learn vital lessons about what to tweak.

Gain Buy-in with Heart-Based Momentum: Storytelling

I n 2008, when we first started in the trenches building VEEV, we always asked customers what had led them to buy our product. We heard a lot of answers, from enjoying the taste and perceiving the brand as cutting edge and cool to being intrigued by the bottle and seeing the product as an affordable luxury with a sustainable mission.

This past year, while we were at the Natural Products Expo West, the largest food and beverage show for natural products in the world, we found ourselves continuing to ask consumers about their purchasing decisions. Either out of curiosity or habit or both, we still like to understand what drives consumers to buy what they buy. We were both surprised by what we heard. Repeatedly, customers told us that they wanted to know where brands stood on various issues, including politics. "But you're buying popcorn," we thought. "Why does it matter which political candidate a brand supports?"

We thought back to 2008, also an election year, racking our brains to remember if that had been an issue then. Barack Obama was running for president for the first time, and we remembered the tangible political energy. But neither of us could remember a single instance when consumers had wanted to know where VEEV stood politically. Eight years later, consumers are paying attention to different things than they used to. More and more, they are being driven by emotional factors.

This new focus is not an isolated phenomenon, and it has important implications for how you engage your customers, as well as how you think about your internal customers and evangelists—your team. In this chapter, we show you why this trend is occurring and how to use it to connect more meaningfully with your internal and external audiences. By the end, you'll have what it takes to create a companywide movement that will snowball outward, creating what we call heart-based momentum, gathering velocity as it grows.

WHAT YOUR BRAND STANDS FOR MATTERS MORE THAN EVER

Even just a few years ago, when consumers were less overwhelmed by the abundant offerings around them, purchasing decisions were made more rationally: lowest price, fastest delivery time, and so on. But as we pointed out in Switchup 8, more and more of these points of differentiation are being eliminated through commoditization. As a result of this trend, it's the relationship that you develop with your consumers—your brand—that has become the last standing and strongest differentiator you have.

Consumers are now asking questions of brands that businesses have historically not had to answer, such as "For whom and what do you stand? What cause or charitable mission does your company support?" Nowhere is this more true than with Millennials, who are, as a demographic, particularly cause driven. And as the segment grows, what Millennials care about is increasingly important. Millennials are currently the largest demographic in the United States (see the chart opposite) and the one with the most buying power. Estimates project that the country's 90 million–plus Millennials will spend more than $200 billion in 2017. As a result, they have an increasing impact on what is bought and why.

Increasingly, however, no matter what a person's age, the reason for making purchases is emotional. To understand the extent of this shift, a recent study compared the purchase decision process in 1985 to the same process today. According to the study, in 1985, the purchase decision process was 70 percent rational and 30 percent emotional. That means buyers were homing in on factors such as affordability when making decisions. By 2005, buyers were making decisions that were 30 percent rational, 70 percent emotional, and, by 2015, only 20 percent rational and 80 percent emotional. Overwhelmingly, consumers are now making emotional choices influenced by emotional connections.

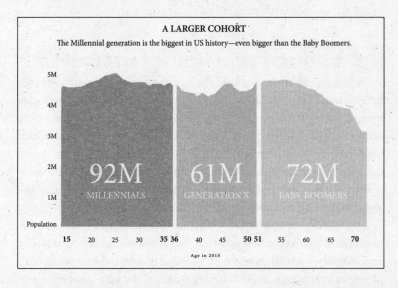

We believe that this shift is being driven by a confluence of factors, including, as we've said, the rise of product and service standards (there are more good options), but also digital media (learning about products and services through social networks as opposed to more traditional channels), as well as by Millennials' cause-driven focus. The chart that follows outlines an additional insight: Millennials' expectations are around 20 percent higher than those of Gen X. That means this trend is only becoming more pronounced.

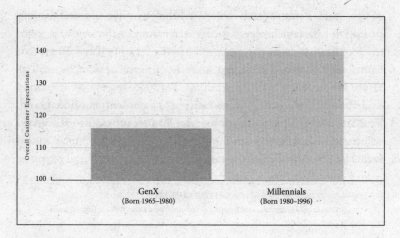

Whatever the reasons behind the transition, such a drastic shift calls for major changes in how brands communicate and connect with customers, both internal (employees) and external (buyers, consumers). In a world where consumers are buying—and employees choosing whom to work for—with their hearts, your brand is more important than it has ever been. It will either resonate strongly or fall short. As companies realize this and spend more time and money attempting to connect with consumers, the competition for "heart share" has increased to new heights. Brands with millions of Facebook, Twitter, and Instagram followers are responding directly to individual consumers on social media. Even founders who have historically been far removed from customers are engaging directly and developing relationships with customers.

As a consequence, many customers today feel that they know the founders of the brands they're interested in, and they develop affinity or loyalty as a result. This experience will only increase as celebrities of all sorts, including famous founders, increasingly turn to artificial intelligence (i.e., chatbots) that can be programmed to give a seemingly personal touch to customer interactions. For instance, the John Mackey chatbot could tweet you to find out what you think of the latest products at Whole Foods Market. Chatbots aside, there are no quick answers to succeeding in this new reality. However, from working with our portfolio companies, we've identified four pillars to establishing meaningful relationships with customers:

1. **Authenticity.** A culture, brand, and set of activities that ring true and are in accordance with your purpose.
2. **Purpose.** Your core and identifiable set of values. A reason for existence beyond the product or service you are providing—the why behind your what.
3. **Storytelling.** The capacity to communicate authenticity and purpose in a compelling and accessible way.
4. **A positive company culture.** The atmosphere you create through authenticity, purpose, storytelling, and other practices that turn employees into key brand ambassadors.

When you develop these four pillars, you create the foundation for successful relationships with employees and customers. Connecting in the right way with all four, where your brand touches more and more people on an emotional level, creates momentum that's heart based. It's a force that will draw more and more like-minded people to you, as well as create the kind of media buzz that fuels today's success.

AUTHENTICITY

Intuitively, entrepreneurs want to target customers using logic and facts, but this no longer cuts it. You must get out of consumers' heads and into their hearts—and we believe that the ability to do so relies on authenticity. Your brand must come from a genuine place, practice what it preaches, and be completely clear about what it is and what it offers customers and employees.

Although authenticity may sound like an attribute unrelated to business success, studies indicate quite the opposite. In the chart on the next page, you will find that Net Promoter Score (NPS), a measure of the likelihood that customers will recommend your brand or product to others, directly correlates with perceived authenticity. Essentially, brands that struggle with authenticity are not recommended by others; they have poor word-of-mouth marketing. Conversely, companies with strong authenticity have a high NPS, which helps with WOM and customer acquisition. High perceived authenticity means not only a better NPS but also a more significant share of high-value customers. In other words, customers spend more on brands that feel authentic.

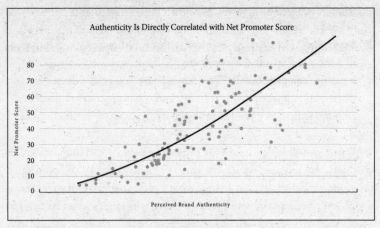

Authenticity Is Directly Correlated with Net Promoter Score

Net Promoter Score

Perceived Brand Authenticity

Though perceived authenticity clearly drives WOM and appears to be an obvious goal for any startup, some companies have chosen to ignore the trend toward authenticity and to focus their spending on their product and its features. Although this may be a more obvious route to driving sales, such companies are actually negatively impacting their NPS and are losing out on an opportunity to connect with customers on an emotional level.

We've found that authenticity comes in many forms. Here we want to highlight three in particular.

Transparency

Brand transparency is the idea that companies are so authentic that they are willing to expose parts of their inner workings to the world. Back in the day, a customer would go to a fast casual restaurant, order a hamburger, eat it, pay for it, and likely never think about where it came from, how the employees were compensated, and what the environmental footprint of the operation was.

These days, there is a growing trend toward transparency. One way brands, especially those that focus on Millennials, win hearts is by finding ways to expose what they are doing. Take Tender Greens, an LA-based high-end fast casual restaurant. Its founders came to realize that consumers wanted to know where their salad ingredients are sourced from—literally down to the name and city of the farm. They began to post the sources of their menu's ingredients on their website and in their restaurants, as well as pictures of the farms the ingredients come from, which were all locally sourced. By allowing the customer to essentially see inside the company, Tender Greens has demonstrated that it has nothing to hide from consumers and is coming from an authentic place.

Integrity

By integrity, we mean a consistency throughout the entire concept—from branding to marketing to products and services. A great example of brand integrity is GT's Living Foods, which was started by our old friend GT Dave, originally out of his effort to help improve his mom's health. Since founding the brand in his parents' kitchen, GT Dave has maintained exceptional standards and a consistent mission of spreading the healing benefits of kombucha and other foods. Visit the brand's website or look closely at its product labels, and you'll feel the sense of community that has been integral to the brand from day one.

Social Good

One company that has been light-years ahead of others in meeting consumers' new, more emotional expectations is TOMS Shoes. TOMS has created a brand that is so authentic that the business itself has become synonymous with its social mission. The genius behind TOMS's success is its founder, Blake Mycoskie, who was one of the first people we met when we moved to LA. While traveling through Argentina in 2006, he was troubled by the number of shoeless poor children he encountered, and he took on the bold task of putting shoes on their feet.

As an entrepreneur and a humanitarian, Mycoskie went on to create a brand that puts inspiring others above selling products—a concept so innovative and disruptive that companies are still attempting to determine how to follow suit.

TOMS was founded on the principle that it would give back in an impactful fashion. For each pair of shoes sold, TOMS gives a pair of shoes to a child in need. After having distributed more than 70 million pairs of shoes to children in need, TOMS has expanded its charitable focus to include clean water, safe birth, and bullying prevention services.

Today, a host of brands have taken note of TOMS's success and adopted similar models. Though many have tried, those that have a more genuine story have found success resonating with customers. When Skechers saw the success that TOMS was experiencing in the market, it launched BOBS to compete in the space. However, Millennials did not feel connected to the BOBS brand in the way they did to TOMS. TOMS's ability to win on authenticity and emotion was so strong that it prevented a new entrant from stealing market share. It all comes back to authenticity and having a story that resonates with customers.

Another strong example of a brand focused on social good is Thrive Market. Having been raised in a household supported by a single mother, its cofounder Gunnar Lovelace has made social impact a priority for the company. Recognizing that 80 percent of low-income families resort to purchasing food that they know isn't healthful, he set out to "make healthy living easy and affordable for everyone." Part of the way he delivers on his promise is by donating a Thrive membership to a low-income family, teacher, veteran, or student for each paid membership he sells.

Think for a moment about the impact that missions like those of TOMS and Thrive have. First and most important, they directly help people in need and make customers feel that they're making a difference in the world through their purchases. By spreading messages of impact across social channels for everyone to see, their brand stories attract a particular set of employees and customers, as well as celebrities and major PR resources that resonate with their mission. This approach helps to build a community of evangelists, brand supporters, and advocates who can create tremendous momentum. When employees and early advocates tell friends about the company and the amazing impact on the world that the company is having, word of mouth spreads, creating the kind of buzz every startup wants and needs.

PURPOSE

We're not saying that a philanthropic mission is required to attract customers or employees. There are plenty of successful companies that connect with people in other ways. What's essential is not necessarily that you give back but rather that your company have some kind of larger purpose—one that you and those who work for you can believe in, that resonates with customers, and that can be quickly and simply articulated.

Purpose is the "why" of what you are doing. It explains the reason you exist as an organization. Simon Sinek, a successful business marketer and public speaker, has said, "People don't buy what you do, they buy why you do it." We highly recommend checking out his TED talk, which captures the essence of this Switchup: that today people are basing their buying actions on their feelings.

To unleash the power of purpose, you must differentiate the "what," "how," and "why" of your company. Let's use Thrive Market as an example. The "what" is the products or services a company offers. For Thrive, that's a wide variety of nonperishable organic food products sold online. "How" refers to the things about your product or service that make it special or set it apart from your competition. For Thrive, it is the membership option, which includes educational content, grocery stipends, and free memberships. The "why" is the reason you exist—your purpose, cause, or belief. Most companies call it their mission. Technology companies often like to call it a phrase coined by the entrepreneur Peter Diamandis: a massively transformative purpose, or MTP. In Thrive's case, it's "to make healthy living easy and affordable for everyone." Understanding your company's "why" is crucial because it is through articulating and broadcasting that purpose that you create the heart-based momentum you need.

With VEEV, our purpose was to provide consumers a better way to drink. We took that literally, in terms of the product, but also environmentally, as a company committed to protecting the planet. We became certified carbon neutral by Climate Clean, making us the first US alcohol company—and one of the first consumer goods companies—to fully offset the carbon footprint of our business activities. As we mentioned earlier, we also donated $1 of every bottle sold to eco-friendly initiatives in the Brazilian rain forest, to ensure that money went back to where açaí comes from. Our distillery was the only one in the United States to acquire a portion of its power through renewable wind generation, our distillation process used 1/200 the energy of traditional methods, and all of VEEV's marketing and sales materials were printed with soy ink on recycled paper.

This focus on the environment attracted employees who were excited about being part of the first spirits company to be a member of Business for Social Responsibility, as well as media attention that helped drive brand awareness and consumer loyalty. Did we do it perfectly? Of course not. But we were able to set out a clear purpose in the market, and internal and external customers alike responded well.

As we've said, your purpose doesn't have to be philanthropic. A great example of a nonphilanthropic startup with a clear "why" is a business that we are particularly excited about: June. June describes its mission as follows: "To use the power of technology to inspire everyone to cook." Their first product? A computer-based oven that "solves the problem that has challenged cooks for years—unpredictable cooking. Now you can cook your food exactly how you want it, no guesswork required." Pretty cool, right?

Having a clear purpose is also crucial for individual and team motivation. As the bestselling business author Daniel Pink pointed out in his book *Drive: The Surprising Truth About What Motivates Us*, working for a purpose you believe in is one of the three key human motivators, above and beyond financial compensation. (The other two, he wrote, are mastery—the chance to get better and better at something—and autonomy—the freedom to do things the way you want to.) Connecting to a larger purpose not only fuels greater effort but fosters enhanced creativity and innovative thinking, two qualities that entrepreneurs need from employees. Overall, research on successful teams shows that when there is a high clarity of purpose, both teams and individuals thrive. Because it's such a powerful motivator, the "why" of your company is one of the key differentiators you have to attract and retain talented employees and partners.

Five Steps to Articulating Your "Why"

1. Bring your leadership team or cofounders together for an off-site for at least a couple of hours. If it's just you, that's fine, too. Don't overthink this. Individually write your answer on a sticky note to the following questions: Why do we exist as a company? What's our mission/vision/purpose/passion/MTP? FYI, some folks get hung up about words such as "mission" and "massively transformative purpose." Adjust your question to your group's mind-set.

2. Get visual: Write on sticky notes, post them on the wall, and arrange them around common themes. Discuss them until you have something that feels right.

3. Is your idea clear? Does it create a "Heck, yeah!" feeling? Can you imagine saying this over and over and still being excited? Here's ours for M13: "To leverage our experience, access, and unique advantages to dramatically accelerate the growth of businesses."

4. Try it out on prospective clients, employees, partners, and customers to see what their responses are.

5. Use it as the north-star question to evaluate organizational decisions. For instance, at M13, we ask ourselves, "Will this opportunity or idea help us leverage our experience, access, and unique advantages to dramatically accelerate the growth of businesses?"

Once you've landed on your purpose, everyone who partners and works with you should be bought into it and talking about it to everyone they know—online and off-line. That takes us to pillar number 3, storytelling.

STORYTELLING

Unfortunately, it's not enough to have authenticity and purpose if no one hears about them. You need to get your story out there. As you've probably noticed, storytelling has recently become even more central to brand building. You can't really build your brand without having customers buy into your story.

How good are you at describing and getting people excited about what you're doing? So much of creating heart-based momentum comes from your ability as a founder to inspire others. From our vantage point at M13, we've seen a number of great ideas go unfunded because the founders were unable to win over the hearts and minds of investors. When we're unimpressed with a founder's story, we can only assume that the company's employees also have trouble buying in.

Storytelling should come from the reason your business exists, why you developed the products or services you did. That is the story customers want to hear. Typically, founders talk about the "what" first ("We're an on-demand laundry service") rather than the "why" ("We want to remove boring chores from your home and life"). See the difference? The first is factual. As research in the beginning of this chapter indicates, factual appeals probably won't move you to buy. The second is engaging and stimulates a reaction. Because you want to engage with customers' hearts, you should make the "why" front and center in the way you communicate. A good story will make you stand out, the buyer will never forget you, and that will pay off in the long run.

Sir Kensington's, a high-quality condiment company, is an example of a brand that found tremendous momentum through great storytelling that, through humor, identified its brand as playful, creative, and innovative. Brown University students Scott Norton and Mark Ramadan had been talking about creating a better ketchup since 2008. Finally, in 2010, with a fictitious origin story that attracted a great deal of attention, they launched their line of condiments. Their storytelling was creative and unique—and although the story was not historically true, their authenticity was demonstrated through the humor in their writing style: they claimed to have discovered the spice chronicles of a Sir Kensington in Brown University library's special collections. Sir Kensington, they wrote, advised the British East India Company in the speculation of rare spices and later became an entrepreneur, selling his business to Lloyds of London and turning to hosting salons, "quickly realizing that the secret to a pleasing gathering was the gastronomic fuel on which it ran," as they say in their official story. "At one such summit, the emperor of Japan presented the assembled guests with tender slices of Wagyu beef. Upon being served, Catherine the Great of Russia leaned toward Sir Kensington to request a side of ketchup. Baffled yet intrigued by the request, Kensington ventured to the kitchen, where he could find nothing acceptable for such a dish or such a diner. Undeterred, he set about to create, on the spot, a ketchup that would forever bear his name. And so the knowledgeable knight became a ketchup king, forever to be fondly favoured for his flavourful findings. He remains to this day the only commoner to have been invited to Buckingham Palace for three meals in a single day."

Charming story, right? You can imagine that they perfected it over time, using it not only for their website but for publicity. "You can't take yourself too seriously" when working with condiments, Mark commented in an article in *The Street*.

Their story doesn't end there—for here's where the momentum they created really paid off. Our friend Rohan Oza, the former CMO of Vitaminwater, was walking the supermarket aisle one day, thinking about the rise of the better-burger movement, when he realized that people were going to pay a lot for fancy burgers and not want to put plain old Heinz ketchup on them. Someone was going to do the better ketchup, and there will be a huge market. He'd heard about Sir Kensington's and decided it had what it took to be the one. He immediately invested in the company.

The Structure of a Great Story

If you're not a great storyteller like the Sir Kensington's founders or Blake Mycoskie, we strongly suggest that you partner with someone who can help you. One of the main experts in the field is Nancy Duarte. In a famous TED talk, she explained that powerful speeches have a specific structure: First they remind people of the status quo or the problem, what she calls the "what is." Then the rest of the speech is an effort to bridge the gap to the future, playing up the contrast between "what is" and the ideal state, the "what could be."

This means that you don't need to go into too much detail about the features of your product or service. Rather, you want customers to get a picture of the wonderful future state that is possible with your idea, service, or product. For instance, the Warby Parker story about donating glasses to nonprofit partners and training people in developing countries to give eye exams and sell glasses at affordable prices, paired with some specific success stories, is quite captivating.

Similarly, you shouldn't get hung up on explaining the details of price point or packaging. Explain your mission, maybe tell a few individual stories or anecdotes that help bring it to life, and end with a short, simple call to action. This is what Duarte calls "the new bliss"—how better listeners' lives would be if they did what you want them to do.

Great Storytelling Starts Internally

The momentum you create through storytelling should initially happen within your company and then be broadcast outward. If the guts of your brand—your employees—haven't bought into the story, it won't have a chance with customers. Being inclusive and inviting everyone from your first employee to be part of your story can help improve it.

Once you have employee buy-in, like-minded customers will quickly follow. That's what happened for Blake Mycoskie. He's won the hearts of millions, but it started with his employees. He first won over a group of interns, who were willing to work for free out of his apartment because they believed in what he was doing. Those interns then broadcast their enthusiasm to their friends through social media, which won the hearts of a few key buyers in stores in Venice, California—and eventually of Nordstrom's buyers. As the TOMS story spread, the momentum built and the company was eventually featured in an AT&T commercial, introducing his "Buy one, give one" model to the world.

POSITIVE COMPANY CULTURE

Whereas companies used to have a "customer first" mind-set, today brand building begins internally, with employees. This is not because startups don't appreciate their customers, or customers are more easily satisfied today than in the past—they're actually more difficult to please. Rather, it is because if you don't get your employees' engagement, support, and buy-in, you'll never get your customers'.

When you are in startup mode, asking your people to work long hours, you need your employees to buy into your mission and live and breathe the brand. They are out there on the front lines interacting with customers. That means you need to make sure that your company is a healthy, vibrant place to work, so that your employees become your key brand advocates.

Culture is not something you set once, like a policy. It cannot run on autopilot. It requires constant focus. It needs attention daily, monthly, quarterly. The minute you stop focusing on it, it quickly drifts away.

One company that has fundamentally changed the way that startups think about company culture is Airbnb. Ranked number one on Glassdoor's Best Places to Work 2016, Airbnb is at the forefront of providing employee experiences that not only increase happiness, engagement, and retention but expand on the brand's storytelling. The publicity that Airbnb has received not just on its external customer-facing brand but on its internal employee-facing one is unprecedented. Airbnb, a hospitality company, offers its employees gym access, free massages, gourmet food, and a host of other work experiences that support them physically, emotionally, and intellectually. Can you see the authenticity in this culture?

Your culture is an extension of your brand. The more your culture and your brand are aligned, the more you will attract like-minded customers and partners. What image do you want to project? That will determine the kind of culture you create. Is it super family friendly with babies in the office because you are a baby products company and everyone who works for you is a new mom? We're big huggers and casual dressers—it's just who we are, even when meeting with bigwigs in New York. Those things are a reflection of our brand—Millennial casualness, emphasis on results more than form, blurring the lines between personal life and work.

When it comes to thinking about culture, we're fans of Rob Kaplan, former vice chairman at Goldman Sachs and currently the president and CEO of the Federal Reserve Bank of Dallas. He's written a number of great books on leadership, and one of the things he says is that culture is not something you put on a wall; it's something that emerges as a result of the way you operate from day to day. If you get those things wrong and then try to make up for them by taking your employees bowling once a month, you're not creating a thriving culture.

We agree. Whether you have one employee or a thousand, your company culture is created much more by your example than anything else. This is partially because people learn how to act from you as the founder. It is important to set an example for your employees, because they're an important extension of your brand.

We're also big believers in social good and encourage you to think about a culture that motivates people beyond money and perks. If you are too narrowly focused on those things, you lose a crucial opportunity to develop more passionate engagement on everyone's part, especially Millennials'. Just as consumers are buying for more emotional reasons, so are employees picking companies on factors other than just the highest pay. With work consuming so much more of our hearts and minds beyond nine-to-five, employees are making choices about whom to work for based not just on money but on culture and purpose.

In this very transparent time, with companies like Glassdoor posting comments by unhappy employees and former employees, how you treat your people matters more than ever. What kind of culture you create, the behaviors you encourage and reward—they're all open to public scrutiny in ways they never were before. Every company has its critics, that's only natural, but you want to minimize them as much as possible. The last thing you want is a Facebook campaign against your company because of something you've done or neglected to do.

Below are a few additional items that we think are key to company culture, which our dad always made sure to reinforce.

Share Momentum Internally

Make sure that you share and celebrate small victories with your staff. This will not only rally the troops behind your cause but also spread positivity throughout the organization. On a regular basis, we keep our M13 team abreast of the positive things that are happening as a result of their hard work. Whether you do that with a thermometer chart that shows how you are doing against quarterly goals or an email listing the wins of the week, highlighting your small wins helps to keep motivation high. It gives employees something to broadcast externally as well. There are lots of hard times in the world of startups. Celebrating the little wins and bringing everyone together can keep people feeling that they're advancing toward the goalpost and eager to do more.

This is not only important at small young companies, but also at large successful corporations. Lloyd Blankfein, the CEO and chairman of Goldman Sachs, does it extremely well. He consistently emphasizes the importance of camaraderie within Goldman Sachs and on calls and through emails often praises specific people and teams responsible for wins for the firm.

Clarify Ideal Employee Attributes

Another way to create a powerfully positive culture is by being explicit about the behaviors you expect. Some companies call these competencies. Others frame them as values. Our dad called them key attributes. In 2000, he joined a struggling midwestern manufacturer called Amsted Industries that is 100 percent owned by its employees. An employee stock ownership plan (ESOP) company like this one demands heart-based buy-in. Indeed, it is built on it. Dad put people first and paid the most attention to the kinds of people he brought into the organization. Years ago, he wrote down the key attributes he felt drove success at Amsted. We believe they are examples of unchanging qualities that will stand the test of time, regardless of how fast brands are scaling or where technology is going.

Dad broke his key attributes into three buckets: personal, which applied to everyone in the organization; management, which were for those who oversaw others; and leadership, for those who run the organization. There are all kinds of lists like this. We like his, because they get to the heart of what's needed in only thirteen categories. We've seen lists as long as twenty-five or thirty. That's too much! We encourage you to take his list and use it for your company. In creating a hiring scorecard, you can rank people on a scale of 1 to 10 on each of these. Ditto for turning these into a simple annual or semiannual evaluation form.

You can also use the list as a way to recognize folks by calling out people publicly for exemplifying one of these attributes in their work. People want to feel recognized, they want to provide for their families, and overwhelmingly, they want to be successful. Dad always saw his job, as we see ours, as helping employees be successful and pointing out when they are. Whether it's a small company or a more established startup, boosting morale by recognizing accomplishments never hurts.

Personal Attributes

- **Integrity.** Continuously demonstrating personal and business ethics and values and pushing this behavior throughout the organization.
- **Intelligence.** Quickly understanding the implications of issues and able to take learning from one situation and apply to another.
- **Maturity.** Demonstrating qualities, traits, and demeanor that command respect: courage (willingness to offer views/ideas), dealing with adversity, candor, adaptability, flexibility, emotional IQ.
- **Energy.** Having passion; demonstrating the physical and mental stamina necessary to meet challenges.

Management Attributes

- **Business acumen.** Understanding and utilizing global events, economic, financial, and industry data to accurately diagnose business strengths, weaknesses, and opportunities; identifying key issues and developing plans.
- **Ability to organize to get the job done.** Staffing, people selection.
- **Ability to cope with ambiguity and complexity.** Demonstrating the ability to understand, clarify, and manage ambiguous and complex issues/circumstances.
- **Good decision making.** Analytical (securing relevant information and identifying key issues); committing to an action after developing alternative courses and considering resources, constraints, and organizational values. Making tough, timely decisions.
- **Effective execution.** Getting the job done; problem solving; driving for results; exercising control—setting high goals, using measurement; accountability; tenaciously working to meet or exceed goals; continuously improving themselves and the business.

Leadership Attributes

- **Ability to set a direction.** Clearly establishing goals and objectives; conceptualizing issues and solutions; anticipating.
- **Ability to energize others.** Motivating and inspiring; delegating and empowering, but knowing when to step in; sharing credit and collaborating; providing timely coaching, guidance, and feedback to help others excel on the job and meet key accountabilities; communicating with impact; accessibility; keeping bureaucracy to a minimum.
- **Ability to align people and team development.** Using appropriate methods and interpersonal skills to develop, motivate, and guide a team toward successful outcomes and attainment of business objectives; attracting and retaining top talent.
- **Ability to cope with change.** Continuously seeking or encouraging others to seek opportunities for different and innovative approaches to addressing organizational problems and opportunities.

Lessons from John: Five Things
Great Leaders Say to Their People

John Replogle, the storied consumer products CEO and one of our most valued mentors, has helped build brands from Guinness to Burt's Bees to Seventh Generation. In addition to having a great sense for scaling companies, he's taught us even more about leadership—especially trust, humility, and accessibility. Here are some of the things we've learned from John's guidance:

1. "I trust you to do this." People work harder for leaders who trust them, and making that explicit creates loyalty. You want them to move fast, not worry about checking with you on everything. This should be easy to say; if you don't trust them, they shouldn't be working for you.
2. "When you did X, the effect on me/us/the project was Y." People work for praise, but simply saying "Good job" isn't sufficient. You need to tell the person what exactly he or she did and what positive effect it had. This has the effect of reinforcing that behavior, so the person will do it even more.
3. "I screwed up." When you take ownership of your mistakes, you create a culture where you learn from failure, rather than avoiding or hiding from it.
4. "It's okay that you screwed up, let's figure out how to fix it." You have tremendous power here to set the tone for a "fail fast" culture by how casually you deal with mistakes. Get angry or blame, and people will become cautious and risk averse.
5. "Be sure to come to me if you have any questions or need anything to get this done." You don't want people to get stalled because they're afraid to ask for help.

LIGHTS, CAMERA, ACTION

Once you've honed your ability to capture people's hearts and minds through authenticity, your folks are jazzed about your purpose and the awesome culture you're creating together, and you've developed an interesting and unique story, it's time to get the word out to create momentum.

If you've done a good job of engaging your employees, they're probably already out there in the market spreading your brand's story. And hopefully, you're broadcasting your progress to the types of people you want to attract, whether they are funders, partners, potential hires, or customers. You email a big retailer such as Walmart, saying, "We sold X units in your tier 1 stores last month." Or send an email to distributors with key wins, new account successes, and sales metrics.

Unfortunately, there is no magic formula when it comes to creating momentum. If you follow the steps we've outlined, you'll certainly connect with your customers on an emotional level. That said, here are a few additional strategies to get the snowball rolling.

Make Sure Your Customers Are Hearing About You in the Right Places

We talked in the beginning of the book about becoming clear who is your ideal customer/user. Now it's time to go out and find him or her. That means strategically allocating your marketing budget to optimal channels. This will ensure that you get attention from the places, both virtual and real, where your customer spends time.

As we've said earlier, don't underestimate the power of momentum on a micro scale. You don't need everyone to know about you—just the people you are targeting (ideally, those who love what you're doing). Luckily, social media allow marketers to personalize advertising. For example, a given company's Facebook ads may vary dramatically, depending on the target customer.

Part of how we did this with VEEV, as we've said, was through parties in the LA area. We mapped our target customers' journey and made sure we were everywhere that they were: from nightclubs and parties to grocery stores and restaurants. We strongly believed that having a hundred people who really understood our brand and story was better than having a thousand who knew us a little bit.

Find Places to Tell Your Story

More than ever before, entrepreneurs have opportunities to tell their stories and those of their companies. Channels through which to speak to customers used to be limited, but today you can write a blog, post on social media, speak on a panel, make a video, have coffee with an influencer . . . the list of possibilities is virtually endless.

You should be thinking about how you can do that, as well. Speak with a writer for your local paper, or connect to the influencers who have the most followers on Pinterest in your category. Get out there and spread the word, because if you don't do it, no one else will. It's your job as a founder. So get out there, find audiences that your message will resonate with, and create the heartfelt momentum you need.

PART 3
EXITING

Success Doesn't Equal a Successful Exit: Strategic Sales

I t was 2016, and we'd recently reformulated the original VEEV recipe. Four years before, in 2012, we'd expanded beyond the initial core VEEV Spirits brand to include VitaFrute Cocktails by VEEV, which had helped to nearly double our size. Shortly thereafter, our business that we'd spent years grinding to build was acquired by Luxco, a leading producer, importer, and marketer of alcohol products. It was a momentous end to a long journey. But even being acquired was no walk in the park.

If you're like most entrepreneurs, you'd like to at least have the option to sell your company one day. This Switchup offers some advice and specific tactics to increase the likelihood of that positive outcome.

In the past, if you created a successful company, you could pretty well be assured that you could find a buyer when you wanted to. Today, since there are so many more businesses, it's possible to create a successful company that no one wants to buy. Reality check: yes, you can do everything right, have luck on your side, and build a successful, even profitable business, then have no buyer. *What?*

Just as the forces of globalization, lower barriers to entry, and technological developments are impacting the way you build your business, the same forces are impacting the way people think about buying businesses. As much as these factors are creating opportunities for innovation, they're also creating uncertainty about the future. A less certain future makes it harder to make massive investments that might pay off a decade from now.

In a time of less prolific business creation, there were plenty of buyers for almost any given successful company. You might buy a restaurant or a hardware store that had a steady customer base and a relatively predictable cash flow. Today, given the rate of change and especially new distribution platforms such as Amazon, cash flows are less guaranteed. On the whole, there may not be less merger and acquisition activity, but what's clear is that in most businesses, your cash flow alone is not enough to attract a purchaser. In some way, shape, or form, you need to be strategic to your acquirer. In other words, there needs to be a reason for your business to exist not just today but into the future.

That's the crux of this Switchup—to think about the potential strategic opportunities your business offers and make sure you are focusing on them. To do that, we explain why Luxco bought us and what we learned in the process. Then we'll turn to the typical categories of strategic opportunities, as well as specific ways to prepare for a successful exit. Ideally you're considering these factors from the start. But even if you are several years into your business or contemplating a sale soon, you can take advantage of this Switchup to make your business as attractive an opportunity as possible.

TO REPEAT OURSELVES: START WITH THE END IN MIND

At the beginning of this book, we talked about starting with the end in mind. It's one of Stephen Covey's principles from *The 7 Habits of Highly Effective People*. We think this concept applies as much to selling your company as it does to building your character or your company. What's your end goal?

Fundamentally, entrepreneurs build businesses for one of two reasons: for lifestyle, by which we mean to support them or augment their income over the long haul, or for enterprise value, where all the value is captured at the exit. Building for enterprise value is riskier; there's no guarantee of success, but it offers a potentially (much) higher reward. This decision can sometimes be one of preference or industry, but it requires careful thinking. It affects a number of crucial decisions about how you will grow along the way. For instance, you shouldn't take cash out of your business if you're building for enterprise, because every penny should be spent on increasing value.

With VEEV, we had to build for enterprise value. That's because, in certain businesses, the liquor business being one of them, sales and marketing are such a massive part of ongoing growth. Incurring losses is a natural part of scaling, especially in the early days. As a result, the liquor business would make a terrible lifestyle business. Building for enterprise value meant we had to focus on growing top-line sales, proving that there was strong brand affinity, especially within a particular demographic, and showing that a larger sales force could scale sales. Being able to demonstrate those things was what set us up for an eventual exit, and they were very much on our minds from the early days.

If you don't want to sell and are instead building for cash flow, you need to consider whether you have a business in which you can be a small player and survive in a day and age of large companies. Smaller businesses often have trouble competing with larger companies, which have big budgets and more resources. Think of all the mom-and-pop bookstores that went out of business in the face of Amazon. A key question to consider is: Can you exist in a gap where smaller folks can survive because the big guys won't be going there?

Conversely, if you plan to sell, you need to think about what size you need to achieve or what proof of concept you need to get to in order to be sold. Often you need to reach a certain size to prove that you're a stable acquisition. And you absolutely must be able to answer this question: Who would buy you, and why would they want you? That's the basis of becoming a desirable strategic acquisition target: giving a prospective purchaser a compelling strategic reason to purchase you. To create a sale when you want it, you must provide something of value to the buyer beyond revenue—something that's easier for them to buy than to build.

WHAT ARE BIG COMPANIES BUYING THESE DAYS?

Below are some of the elements big companies are strategically buying for. As you read them, keep in mind what your business might be able to offer.

- **Your distribution model.** Unilever paid $1 billion for Dollar Shave Club. Was it because it thought the market for razors was so huge? Partly. Really it was because it wanted a direct-to-consumer distribution channel, and Dollar Shave Club had created a very successful one. Unilever must have figured that if Dollar Shave Club could do $200 million in revenue largely off one product, it had fervent and loyal customers who could be sold other Dollar Shave Club and even Unilever products really effectively through this channel.
- **Your platform.** Microsoft bought LinkedIn for $26 billion. All kinds of pundits speculated on the reasons why at the time. Among the most compelling is that LinkedIn is fundamentally a content-publishing platform. Microsoft can leverage it with existing products and use it for cross-marketing purposes to reach new customers or existing customers with new products.
- **Your talent.** Walmart bought Jet.com for $3 billion, with many folks arguing that one of the biggest premiums in the sale was Marc Lore, Jet.com's cofounder and CEO and a former leader at Amazon. Following that acquisition, Walmart bought Bonobos for $310 million and said that CEO Andy Dunn, who had helped to build digitally native brands, was a big part of the draw. If Walmart wants to survive, it needs to compete successfully against Amazon, and since Lore had built Jet.com up as a successful direct competitor to Amazon, Walmart valued his talent. With a five-year vesting schedule, Walmart has made an attempt to keep Lore around for a

while. An open question remains: Who will eat whose lunch? Will Walmart be able to attack Amazon's business, or will Amazon take out Walmart's? Amazon's recent acquisition of Whole Foods Market is certainly a shot across the Walmart bow and indicative of the increasingly intertwined worlds of online and off-line commerce.

- **Your technology.** Fossil Group recently paid $250 million for Misfit, a creator of beautiful wearable tech products, largely because of the technology it had created. Misfit's fitness trackers and smartwatches provided Fossil with a new strategic opportunity by implementing its tracking technology in a number of other brands.

- **Your access to a new demographic.** In 2007, when Clorox approached its centennial birthday, the company was aware that a change was necessary. The company noticed that with shifting demographics, Millennial customers were looking for healthy, safe, natural, sustainable products. In order to better target that demographic, Clorox acquired Burt's Bees, an Earth-friendly natural skin care company, for more than $900 million. We're seeing acquisitions like this occur more and more as large corporations scramble to access Millennials. Similar moves have been made by Nordstrom in acquiring the direct-to-consumer apparel company Trunk Club in an attempt to reach new audiences and leverage its existing infrastructure. As Brian Spaly did with Trunk Club, you can build your business strategically, keeping in mind what corporations are having a hard time accessing. In Trunk Club's case, Brian appealed to consumers' desire for a stylish wardrobe without having to shop for it. In that way, it became the perfect acquisition target for a retailer grasping for ways to reach younger consumers with new purchasing behaviors.

- **Your brand.** Sometimes what you are selling to a buyer is less tangible than a technology or talent pool. This is the case with your brand. Though an empty brand can't sell, sometimes what strategic buyers are looking for is a strong brand to get behind. That was the case in the acquisition of Hostess Brands, the American snack and confectionery company. After Apollo Global Management and Metropoulos & Co. purchased Hostess's cake business out of bankruptcy in 2013 for $400 million, the snack company was sold to the publicly traded Gores Group. Alec Gores, the chairman and CEO of the Gores Group, said in a statement, "Hostess presents a unique opportunity to invest in an iconic brand with strong fundamentals that is poised for continued growth." Hostess Brands has since seen a resurgence, with its stock price climbing from $12 in December 2016 to $16 in February 2017.

BECOMING A STRATEGIC PURCHASE

Of course, you're going to try to build a strong brand, a unique distribution model, and innovative technology and hire top talent. That is all important and easier said than done, but the key here is to figure out the reason you think you will be bought. Then obsess over it to strengthen that element as much as possible. For instance, Luxco bought our company because of the brand identity and demographic it gave them access to. Here's how David Bratcher, Luxco's president and COO, put it when announcing the purchase: "VEEV and VitaFrute's premium quality, progressive positioning and commitment to sustainability resonate with today's millennial drinkers."

From the very start, we assumed that brand identity and the Millennial target market would be our compelling reason to be bought. We knew we couldn't build a competing distribution platform; it already existed. And we didn't see a valuable tech play. Once we figured that out, we obsessed over building as strong a brand identity as possible.

You need to do the same: identify where you have a competitive advantage or where you think you can really differentiate yourself. Then make strategic choices to enhance that element. For instance, if you think your most valuable asset will end up being your brand, then when you're allocating your limited budget, you should think about spending more on marketing and making your brand more differentiated and less on, for instance, trying to maximize sales.

Most startups don't differentiate between sales and marketing enough, but there are plenty of ways to prioritize one over the other, allowing you to home in on your goal. If you think a buyer will be attracted to the unique access that you have created to a new or hard-to-reach demographic, you shouldn't spend money or energy trying to attract other customer segments. Instead, focus on that demographic. Strive to be the best company that caters to that particular demographic. That way, prospective buyers will see you as the player with the best access to that group and find value in your company.

To make themselves an attractive acquisition target, many entrepreneurs focus too much effort on increasing sales. Though increased sales may change the price for which you sell your company, it is unlikely to impact whether or not your company is acquired. In terms of being acquired, it's all about increasing your strategic fit and creating an attractive offering to bigger players.

Thinking strategically about the appeal of your business should be an ongoing activity from the start that you ramp up further a few years before you sell. Most corporations are, understandably, not as forward thinking and have less awareness of the startup market. Because of this, it's important to demonstrate your value in advance of your attempted sale. Here are four important factors to consider to position yourself strategically for a successful sale.

Be a Threat

Many startups find success but don't make enough of an impact in their respective industries to be threatening. When your company is truly a concern of more established players, that's when you're in a position to sell, and for a meaningful price. But if your company has found relative success without disrupting anyone and you aren't a threat, it's less likely that you'll achieve a valuable exit. Typically, the way to threaten a bigger player is to start chipping away at its customer base in a way that matters more and more to it. As we've mentioned earlier, the better you know your customers and those of your competitors, the better you'll be able to win their business.

We've seen this quite a bit with apparel companies. There are people who manufacture beautiful, stylish, comfortable clothes, footwear, and accessories and in some cases get to $20 million or even $30 million in sales. That is a lot of money and not easy to achieve. The problem is that even at those revenue levels, there's very little stopping brands such as Zara or Urban Outfitters from replicating your designs. These sales can thus be hard to protect. Furthermore, your brand might be doing meaningful sales but making no real dent in the sales of Nordstrom or Amazon (which is now selling more clothes than Macy's).

If you're not threatening another company and could be replicated with relative ease, it's hard for a prospective buyer to justify paying a large multiple of revenue for your business. You may have built a successful business but may still struggle to find a successful exit.

Build an Affordable House in an Expensive Neighborhood

Have you ever heard the real estate slogan "Be the cheapest house on the nicest block"? It works in business, too. For a good strategic sale, you want to be in an industry with as many potential buyers as possible. The more people who can and want to buy you, the more they'll fight to do so and ultimately drive your purchase price up. Ironically, if you build your business to a point where you're the second or third largest in the industry, you may have created a massive success but missed your opportunity to sell. Who can afford to buy you? If selling is your goal, be aware of the number of potential buyers at any given stage and the inflection point of possible suitors. An optimal point to sell may be when you're the most attractive to the largest number of potential acquirers.

Be Mindful of Capital Efficiency

When it comes to selling your business, one of the most overlooked concepts is capital efficiency. Two businesses that sell for $50 million each are not necessarily equal. It comes down to the amount of time it took and, crucially, the amount of capital that was invested over the life of the business. Similar to the example we discussed in the introduction, the same sale price can have materially different outcomes for investors and founders alike.

Imagine that each of two businesses is acquired for $50 million. The first raised $30 million in capital, whereas the second, for a combination of reasons, was able to raise only $5 million. Putting time aside, the first business yields 1.6 times invested capital. Imagine sinking five to seven years of your heart and soul into a business. Would you be happy with a 1.6-times return? Possibly, depending on other factors. On the other hand, take the second business, which was also sold for $50 million, but after raising only $5 million, yielding a 10-times ROI, a home run by most standards.

There's a lot of hype around the sale number—the top line. Make sure you're focused on that, but pay equal attention to growing in the most capital-efficient way possible. Using the above example, with the same amounts of capital raised, we'd rather invest in the second business, even if it sold for $10 million, $40 million less than the first business, because that would provide a 2-times return ($10 million divided by $5 million) compared to a 1.6-times return ($50 million divided by $30 million). Your capital efficiency will impact the amount of money that ultimately ends up in your and your investors' pockets!

Establish Relationships with Potential Buyers Early On

Selling to a company that hasn't been involved with you in the past, as we did with VEEV, is a possibility, of course. But it's much easier to sell if you've already warmed up the relationship through some kind of previous alliance. Chances are, if you have created the kinds of partnerships we talked about in Switchup 4, your buyer might be someone you are already doing business with. Or someone who has already invested in your company.

It's increasingly common for large companies and corporations to first invest in startups before acquiring them. This strategy allows them to hedge their bets and to see what a business is capable of and what potential it has for the future. Nordstrom, for example, has frequently invested in brands that it later acquired. Similarly, large media companies are investing in small social media companies with an eye toward eventual purchase.

PepsiCo's relationship with KeVita is a good example. Pepsi decided to "rent with an option to buy" KeVita. Several years prior to the outright acquisition of KeVita, Pepsi made a sizable investment, helped with some select distribution, and became a board observer in the company. That gave the Pepsi team a chance to get to know the KeVita management well, understand the product, and, just as important, block potential suitors such as Coca-Cola or Dr Pepper Snapple Group from having a first look at KeVita when the time came to sell.

If you haven't yet considered this, now is the time to begin to look for and develop relationships with strategic partners and investors. Think about who would be a strategic buyer and make sure that you are on their radar. Make them feel special—while protecting your IP and leveraging their infrastructure, of course.

WHEN TO SELL

At the most basic level, when we started, we said we thought we could grow our company to a particular size on our own. And within a pretty close margin, that's about where we got it.

From the start, our goal was always to sell VEEV and give it a chance to endure and succeed through another, larger strategic player within the industry. Working back from that goal was important, because it was the filter we used to make every decision. If we had to sum up the reasons we thought we had to sell VEEV when we did, they would be the following:

First, it was a good time in the macro economy to be selling something. Never underestimate this, as timing can be everything. Take, for example, the purchase of Instagram by Facebook for $1 billion in cash and stock in 2012. In a 2012 blog post, Mark Zuckerberg said the reason was that "Facebook is essentially about photos, and Instagram had found and attacked Facebook's Achilles heel—mobile photo sharing." These days, as we mentioned earlier, Facebook is much more focused on video, so if you had a company that offered something in the photo space today, you might have a hard time getting Facebook's attention. But it's why, in 2014, Facebook paid $400 million to $500 million for the video ad tech startup LiveRail. It's important to be aware of the larger climate in general, as well as what's going on with the big players by which you might be purchased.

Second, we felt that we had gotten VEEV almost as far as we could by ourselves and wanted to sell before growth stalled. It's always good to be selling from a position of demand and interest versus necessity. If you have a good growth trajectory under your belt and aren't sure you can sustain it, it might be a good time to pursue a sale.

Third, we felt the brand could still have a lot of runway with a bigger company, and we wanted someone else to see the value and take it to the next level. Luckily, Luxco did.

There were also a number of other issues that factored into our thinking. First, the industry had continued to evolve in ways that didn't favor us. There was a lot more competition for craft spirits than when we had started. We were caught in a middle place: we were too big to be small but too small to be big. And because of our media success, we were perceived to be bigger than we were. In addition, when we started, white spirits such as vodka were superhot. Then brown and other dark spirits became hot.

Simultaneously, there was a big consolidation of distributors in the industry, which was good for large brands such as Bacardi and Brown-Forman and really not good for small companies. Suddenly there were only five companies paying more than 90 percent of our distributor's bills. Why would distributors spend much time on VEEV when they made most of their money on the big guys? When we started, there were many more distributors who were competing for our business, so we got more of their mind share and time.

All of those factors meant that running the business wasn't as much fun anymore and, more important, we were no longer the best suited to grow it. We'd built it to a particular point, but then the ecosystem had changed and the cards had become more stacked against us.

This is not an uncommon founders' phenomenon. What takes you from point A to point B typically is not what gets you from point B to point C, and you might not be the best suited for that next phase.

With VEEV, we were able to get over our lack of twenty-five-year relationships in the industry with innovation. But to get to the next level, what was needed was very-long-term relationships with big distribution muscle, which we just didn't have.

It takes self-awareness to know what you're best suited for and when to say that someone else is better suited to take your company from here to there. Many entrepreneurs are temperamentally suited for the initial build stage of a company and have less interest or skill in the scale and run phases.

One concept we've started to think more and more about is what we're calling the *start-to-finish* scale. On one end of the spectrum is the energetic visionary who turns an idea into something. On the other end, there's, say, a public company CEO, a true manager and leader who can handle the complexity of a massive, diversified corporation. Different skills and mind-sets are required for various steps of the journey. Occasionally, a transcendent leader can take a company from inception to a successful public operating company. Mark Zuckerberg is one of them, but they are few and far between. Inevitably, the most important thing is knowing where you are best, whom you need to surround yourself with, and when it's time to go.

THE NITTY-GRITTY OF SELLING YOUR BUSINESS

Even if you've been thinking and acting strategically about an exit from the beginning, you can't just wake up one day, decide to sell your business, and do it next week. The process takes time, usually six to twelve months, minimum. For VEEV, once we knew we were ready to sell, we began by identifying about five companies that might be interested in us as a strategic acquisition. Then we started finding reasons to talk to them. Courtney would call one up and say, "I happen to be in Louisville tomorrow, just for the day. Want to get lunch?" We hadn't been planning to be in Louisville. But if they said yes, you better believe we bought seats on the next flight just so we could have an informal conversation. That allowed us to talk about what VEEV was and how we were doing, so that when it came time to announce that we were for sale, these companies had a positive association. That part was fun, but that was not necessarily the case with the whole process. Here are some of our other lessons learned from the trenches of our sale.

Sell the Dream

Tell a compelling story about your company's future, where an acquirer could take the brand from where you've gotten it to: "We've done *xyz* in five states—imagine if you did it in the entire country or even expanded internationally." Play into your potential acquirer's strengths and show it how it can take your company to the next order of magnitude. Sell it on what you're going to give it access to in the process. The better you are at painting an exciting story about what it can do with your company, the more likely it is to bite—and to value your company at a higher price.

Find a Buffer to Create Competitive Tension

You're going to need a great team of advisers to help you through the sale of your company. Depending on your experience, you want to fill any knowledge gaps you have with a team that can advise you on both the legal and business sides of things: an investment banker or business broker, an attorney specializing in mergers and acquisitions, and a seasoned accountant. When considering an investment banker, don't be afraid to negotiate their standard terms (investment bankers tend to favor themselves, obviously), and be sure to check references and dig deep. When it comes to negotiating with buyers, you want to find an investment banker or broker who's able to navigate large and complex organizations, someone who knows potential buyers and has relationships with them.

For instance, if you are being acquired for marketing purposes, you would want the chief marketing officer or a high-level marketing officer in your corner. The person should also come with a track record of winning for entrepreneurs and be willing to get into the middle between you and the buyer to create what we call "competitive tension." Such a representative creates a sense of urgency about the sale of your company and drives demand. This person should really know how to sell and be able to craft the right story that will resonate with the buyer. It's equally important that you have an advocate on the inside, within the company, who has power and has reasons to want to acquire you. Find someone who is going to pound the table for you.

Keep It Quiet

As you go through the sales process, you want to keep your sales plans very close to the vest. You don't want to create uncertainty among your customers, suppliers, or employees, which can devalue your business and make things much more challenging. Make sure that any consultants sign tight confidentiality agreements. There will be time to prep your staff as the sale gets closer.

Be Prepared for the Long Haul

Statistics indicate that one of three deals falls apart in the due diligence process. So don't be too surprised if a deal falls through. It doesn't mean that you won't be able to find another buyer—or even that the folks who walked away won't return at some point. A purchase is a combination of timing and opportunity, so be prepared to hang in there till it's done.

EXIT TO-DOS TWELVE TO EIGHTEEN MONTHS IN ADVANCE

When it comes to a sale, there is a lot that is out of your control. But what's in your control is how far in advance and how well you plan. As Louis Pasteur once said, "Chance favors the prepared mind." Here's how to best prepare your company for a sale:

- **Get your house in order.** This should go without saying, but a lot of people who want to sell their companies wouldn't be able to sell tomorrow even if they wanted to, because all their ducks aren't in a row. It's hard to be specific here, because it depends on your industry, but get that intellectual property in order, straighten out any international issues, any litigation, and so on. If someone is infringing on your patent or trademark, take care of it. Clean up all paperwork and HR issues. There are sites dedicated to generic due diligence requests that can help you with this process.

- **Precourt possible buyers.** We never understood the importance of this until we did it. Unless you're like our friend Brian Lee and people are falling all over you to buy whatever company you start next, most of us have to do a lot of precourting. We thought that because we'd had some success in the industry, buyers would approach us. As it turns out, most people we courted were interested, but consistent engagement on our part was essential to achieving a sale. We recommend having a list of people or companies on your radar as potential buyers and then posting them updates on a regular basis; giving them a window into your momentum will ensure that you are a part of the conversation when they begin having internal conversations about the category or your direct competitors.
- **Highlight the key driver(s) of your acquisition.** Once you determine what you believe the key driver for an acquirer will be, exploit it, emphasize it, and put a shiny red bow on it. Make sure potential acquirers know you have exactly what they are looking for.
- **Understand the hidden costs of sale preparation.** We can't emphasize enough the time, effort, and distraction costs of a sale. It's like building a house: it takes twice as long as you think and costs twice as much. This is in terms of both hard costs and time/resource costs, which are the real killer. Go in with your eyes open, prepare well, and hopefully it will all be worth it in the end.

ENOUGH FROM US—GET AFTER IT!

I t's easy to idealize the process of selling your company. In many ways, it's important to do so. You need a light at the end of the very tough tunnel that's building a company from scratch. This is not a job or life for everyone; it's one of the hardest things you can do. It's a nonstop job with nobody else to blame when things go wrong. It's ever changing, potentially capital and people intensive, and complicated. You can make so many right decisions and still not have it all work out.

That said, building a company is absolutely one of the most rewarding things you can do in your life. Good companies positively impact all of their stakeholders, including their suppliers, their employees, their customers, and the communities in which they operate. It can be extremely lucrative and a ton of fun. If you choose the right people to surround yourself with, operate with integrity throughout the journey, and never stop learning, it's a hard path to beat.

That's what motivates us every day. We love being entrepreneurs, and we think the world needs more of them—more creative problem solvers who are willing to get into the trenches and relentlessly improve everything they touch. To this day, it's the pursuit of excellence through innovation and solving problems that leads to true global change that motivates us to get out of bed and do what we do. We don't just talk about these Switchups; we live them.

We're going to do our best to continue updating our website (www.shortcutyourstartup.com) with relevant resources and new ideas and strategies as the world keeps changing. We hope that you enjoyed this book, but we're even more excited to see the great company you build as you put these ideas into practice. Carpe diem, and get on it!

ACKNOWLEDGMENTS

We always talk about startups being a team sport, and we've discovered that publishing a book is no different. *Shortcut Your Startup* would not have seen the light of day without the hard work of many people, starting with our collaborators MJ Ryan and M13's own Kevin Weiss and Andrew Shein, as well as our fabulous agent, Yfat Reiss Gendell, and her hardworking team at Foundry Media: Jessica Felleman, Sara DeNobrega, Colette Grecco, Kirsten Neuhaus, Heidi Gall, Richie Kern, Molly Gendell, Deirdre Smerillo, Hayley Burdett, and Melissa Moorehead.

Yfat led us to Gallery Books and Jeremie Ruby-Strauss, whose fine editing confirmed to us once again the power of iterating. We want to thank not only him, Nina Cordes, and Brita Lundberg, but the entire Gallery gang, whose efforts have led to the book in front of you: Jen Bergstrom, Jen Long, Louise Burke, Gina Borgia, Jen Robinson, Liz Psaltis, Steve Breslin, Larry Pekarek, Jaime Putorti, Lisa Litwack, John Vairo, Caroline Pallotta, Rachel DeCesario, Abby Zidle, Diana Velasquez, Mackenzie Hickey, Sade Oyalowo, Laura Waters, Irene Lipsky, Caitlin McCreary, and of course Paul O'Halloran and Liz Lotto.

We also cannot express enough our gratitude to our family: our mom, Sherry Reum; our sister, Halle, and her husband, Oliver; and of course Dad, whose inspiration and mentorship in every way laid the foundation for this book. Beyond our immediate family, we want to acknowledge every member of the Reum (#ReumTeam) and Milliken families, both living and no longer with us but who are with us in spirit. You have all influenced and contributed to our success greatly, and we couldn't ask for a more loving group.

We also want to thank our other family, M13. Kevin Weiss, Andrew Shein, and Donna Chindamanee in particular put so much into this book, but every member of our M13 Tribe works so hard and enables us to take on crazy projects like writing a book. Thank you to Erik Tarui, Brian Nicholson, Hondo Tey, and everyone else within the M13 Galaxy.

Lastly, we want to thank our support system . . . you know who you are. From YPO to Tiger 21, coaches, mentors, and friends, we have felt the outpouring of support from every corner of the globe over what has been the most challenging year of our lives but also one of the most rewarding. WE ARE SO GRATEFUL, AND WE LOVE YOU ALL SO MUCH.

INDEX

SOURCES

Graphic elements appearing in text were created based on the following sources (those not listed were generated internally):

page 15: https://www.cbinsights.com/blog/venture-capital-funnel-2/

page 24: Nicholas Felton, "Consumption Spreads Faster Today," *The New York Times*, February 10, 2008

page 38: screen shot from Everlane website

page 50: CNBC, company filings

page 74: https://blogs.wsj.com/moneybeat/2013/09/20/blackberrys-slump -in-4-charts/?mod=e2tw

page 92 (both images): https://cdn2.hubspot.net/hubfs/1955252/SCC_2016 /Startup_Corporate_Collab_2016_Report.pdf

page 147: http://tomtunguz.com/startup-growth-rate-all-time-high/

page 148: http://blog.secondmeasure.com/2015/06/23/nothing-hairy
-about-dollar-shave-clubs-growth/

page 189: U.S. Census Bureau

page 190: http://www.dmnews.com/marketing-strategy/the-millennial
-baby-boomer-divide/article/430556/

page 192: http://www.flashstock.com/blog/6-types-of-content-to-win
-over-millennials